WHO IS
the
HOLY
SPIRIT?

MARC BAKER

TWO BLESSED BEARS PUBLISHING
Bradenton, FL

Who Is the Holy Spirit?
ISBN: (paperback) 979-8-9887462-6-3
ISBN: (eBook) 979-8-9887462-7-0
Copyright © 2024 by Marc Baker
Bradenton, FL 34203

Published by:
Two Blessed Bears Publishing
Bradenton, FL 34203

www.mbmediaministries.net

Contents

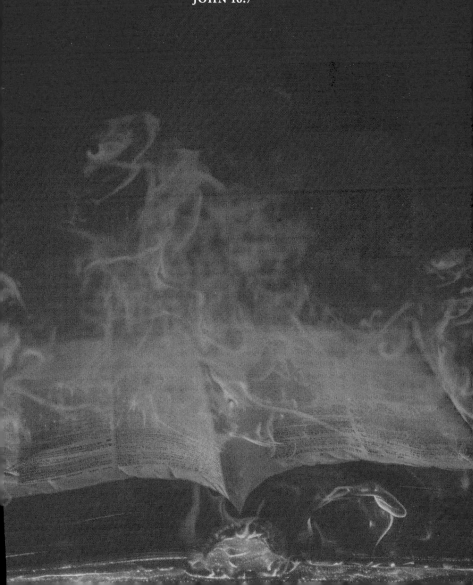

Nevertheless I tell you the truth; It is expedient for you that I go away: for if I go not away, the Comforter will not come unto you; but if I depart, I will send him unto you.

JOHN 16:7

Introduction

In this book, I want to share what I have learned about the Holy Spirit over the past thirty years of walking with Him. There is so much in my spirit to convey about His presence and work in every aspect of our Christian journey.

In Section 1, we will explore the Spirit's role in the new birth and the unique anointing every believer receives from His indwelling presence.

In Section 2, we will explore how the Holy Spirit reveals our spiritual identity, which is rooted in our position in Christ Jesus. I am grateful for the ministry gifts that God has placed within the body of believers and for what we commonly refer to as the gifts of the Spirit. However, I've found that our ability to benefit from these gifts is directly linked to our understanding of who we are in Christ Jesus.

In Section 3, we will discuss the baptism in the Holy Spirit and a stronger anointing that accompanies it. This is the experience that Jesus referred to in His last command to the disciples, found in Acts 1:4-5:

> And, being assembled together with them, commanded
> them that they should not depart from Jerusalem, but wait
> for the promise of the Father, which, saith he, ye have

heard of me. For John truly baptized with water; but YE
SHALL BE BAPTIZED WITH THE HOLY GHOST
not many days hence.

In Section 4, we will explore the language of the born-again spirit,
which is available to all believers who have been baptized with the
Spirit. This gift allows us to pray directly from our spirit and grants
us access to the depths of revelation knowledge that God wishes to
share with all His children.

In Section 5, we will discuss our relationship and fellowship with
the Holy Spirit. Paul speaks of this in 2 Corinthians 13:14:

The grace of the Lord Jesus Christ, and the love of God,
and the communion of the Holy Ghost, be with you
all. Amen.

The term translated as "communion" in this verse can also be
understood as "fellowship" or "partnership." While this concept may
be unfamiliar to many Christians, the Holy Spirit seeks to spend time
with you and cultivate a relationship. He was sent to guide and teach
us, but all too often, He is overlooked.

In Section 6, we will discuss the operations of the Spirit, often
referred to as the gifts of the Spirit. I consider these to be the actions
He performs. We often focus on seeking what He can do for us, rather
than pursuing a deeper relationship with Him.

As you read this book, keep in mind that while there are many fac-
ets to the Spirit's work in our Christian journey, they all stem from the
same Holy Spirit. I believe that once you experience His presence and
the sweetness of His fellowship, you will never desire anything else.

BORN OF THE SPIRIT

Jesus answered and said unto him, Verily, verily, I say unto thee, Except a man be born again, he cannot see the kingdom of God. Nicodemus saith unto him, How can a man be born when he is old? can he enter the second time into his mother's womb, and be born? Jesus answered, Verily, verily, I say unto thee, EXCEPT A MAN BE BORN OF WATER AND OF THE SPIRIT, he cannot enter into the kingdom of God. That which is born of the flesh is flesh; and THAT WHICH IS BORN OF THE SPIRIT IS SPIRIT. Marvel not that I said unto thee, Ye must be born again. The wind bloweth where it listeth, and thou hearest the sound thereof, but canst not tell whence it cometh, and whither it goeth: SO IS EVERY ONE THAT IS BORN OF THE SPIRIT.

JOHN 3:3-8

Chapter 1

Communion
with the Spirit

*The grace of the Lord Jesus Christ, and the love of God, and
the communion of the Holy Ghost, be with you all. Amen.*

2 CORINTHIANS 13:14

More than thirty years ago, I felt stuck in my relationship with God. I attended services at my church, visited other churches, and heard amazing messages, but I never seemed able to receive God's promises for myself. Thankfully, everything changed when I had an experience in which the Holy Spirit first introduced Himself to me on a cold winter day in Claremore, Oklahoma. I had been saved and baptized with the Spirit for several years, but I never experienced God on a personal level before then.

From my personal experience, I can say that without the baptism with the Holy Spirit, the intimacy I've experienced with the Spirit since that day would not have been possible. The revelation of God's Word and the faith victories I've witnessed over the years are all fruit of the time spent communing with the Holy Spirit. I have found that my relationship with Him is the foundation stone on which my entire Christian life rests.

Our Journey with the Spirit

Our focus in this book will be the Holy Spirit, but we will take a different approach. Initially, we will examine the new birth and what it means to be a new creation in Christ Jesus (2 Corinthians 5:17). Next, we will examine the baptism with the Spirit and how it should affect our lives and our relationship with the Holy Spirit. Finally, we will look at how to develop our awareness of His voice and how to partner with Him in ministry to allow the free flow of His gifts in our lives.

There has been a lot of confusion about the Holy Spirit. Some Christians believe we receive all of Him that is available when receiving salvation, while others believe it is not possible to be saved without first receiving the baptism with the Spirit. Still others think we no longer need His ministry or gifts, as they believe we have evolved in our spiritual maturity beyond the need for manifestations of the Spirit. In this book, we are going to address many of the most common religious teachings that rob Christians of the intimacy the Spirit desires with them.

Led by the Spirit

The journey with the Holy Spirit begins with salvation but does not end there. It continues with the baptism in the Spirit and the development of our fellowship with Him, leading us to become conduits for Him to flow through in power. I recognize that there is some resistance to the baptism in the Spirit, but there are many Scriptures supporting the experience, which we will examine.

One of the most difficult things for me in ministry is the lack of awareness about the Holy Spirit I have found when speaking with many Christians. He is such a pivotal part of my life, and I have come to depend on Him in every area. It seems most of the people I speak with in church over the years have never been told they can have a similar relationship with Him. They recognize He is a part of the Godhead but have never been introduced to Him as someone who desires relationship with them.

One of my anchor Scriptures for my relationship with the Holy Spirit is Romans 8:14, which reads, "For as many as are led by the Spirit of God, these are sons of God" (NKJV). The original language for this verse paints the picture of a place of complete dependence on the Spirit. He was sent to reveal Jesus to us and lead us through every step of our Christian journey. Every son and daughter of God should be completely dependent on Him. This dependence is grown in relationship which grows only through time spent meditating in Scripture and fellowshipping with Him.

Our dependence on the Spirit begins with salvation. No human being will ever receive a revelation of Jesus' redemptive work or accept Him as Lord without the help of the Holy Spirit. We have nothing to offer God and would be completely hopeless without the cross. Understanding this though is not possible without first hearing the Word of God and having what we heard revealed to us by the Spirit. This is an aspect of His ministry Jesus described in John 14:26:

> But the Comforter, which is the Holy Ghost, whom the Father will send in my name, HE SHALL TEACH YOU ALL THINGS, AND BRING ALL THINGS TO YOUR REMEMBRANCE, whatsoever I have said unto you.

I have found that those who walk in the power of God grow in their dependency on the Spirit throughout their Christian journey. As our revelation of the Lord in our lives grows, we should lean on Him more and more for all our needs. Our dependence on the Holy Spirit should grow the longer we live as a Christian; this is because our confidence in our natural abilities should become less and less, causing us to lean on Him more as our relationship with Him strengthens.

Religious Tradition or Relationship

Jesus told His disciples religious traditions would make the Word of God powerless in their lives (Mark 7:13). I experienced this growing up in what would be considered an old-line denominational church. My family attended services faithfully, sent me to catechism, and even had me baptized into membership in the church. The congregation viewed me as a Christian, but if I had died, hell would have been my destination.

The congregation I grew up in had many wonderful people who had a desire to serve God. Some were saved, but few believed in healing, deliverance, or in the Holy Spirit as anything more than some mysterious force. If He was mentioned, it was only in passing as a side reference in a song, liturgy, or sermon. Our church basically taught that the only difference between a Christian and a non-Christian was the fact that Christians had their sins forgiven and would not go to hell when they died.

Jesus came to open the door for us to experience an abundant life (John 10:10), but this did not seem like a reality in my life prior to my meeting the Holy Spirit. There was nothing in my experience in life that was anywhere close to resembling an abundant life. I read Scripture, attended services, and did everything my church told me to. However, none of these religious exercises brought any level of permanent change in my life, and the promises I saw in Scripture seemed to be beyond my reach. I did not feel worthy of receiving them because I did not understand that my identity had been changed when I was born again.

As mentioned at the beginning of this chapter, I was essentially saved but stuck, as the saying goes. It wasn't an issue of sin or a cold heart, as there was a hunger for God in my heart, but nothing that I did seem able to satisfy it. This all changed one winter day in Claremore, Oklahoma, as stated earlier, when I had an encounter that lasted more than four hours in which the Holy Spirit introduced Himself to me. He showed me that everything I hungered for could only be found in a relationship with Him.

The New Birth and Baptism

I have heard ministers say that the baptism with the Spirit is more important than the new birth. However, they are wrong. The baptism with the Spirit is simply the next step in our Christian journey that opens the door for intimacy with the Lord and what we most often call the gifts of the Spirit. In my experience, those who reject the baptism tend to struggle in the same way I did prior to my introduction to the Spirit, not experiencing the victorious life that God ordains for all His children to enjoy.

The baptism is not more important than the new birth, and it is not a matter of us receiving one or the other. They are both essential components of the life that God has planned for each of us. We will begin examining the new birth, and the change it brought to our spirits, in the next chapter. We were first introduced to the Spirit when He drew us to Christ resulting in our conversion. For the disciples, this occurred in Jesus' first appearance to them, which is recorded in John 20:22. He breathed the Holy Spirit into their spirits, and they were born again during their meeting.

Jesus appeared to His disciples multiple times over forty days after this first experience before ascending back to the Father (Acts 1:1-3). His last instruction before departing was to wait in Jerusalem for the baptism with the Spirit (Acts 1:4), even though they had already received Him into their spirits when they were born again. This description shows us that there is a distinct experience separate from salvation that the Lord expects us to receive before launching into ministry. We will study this in depth beginning in chapter 14.

For now, let's jump into salvation, which is where we were first introduced to the Holy Spirit and His ministry.

Chapter 2

God Looks at Our Inner Man

Therefore if any man be in Christ, he is a new creature: old things are passed away; behold, all things are become new.

2 CORINTHIANS 5:17

The apostle Paul tells us that every person "in Christ" is a "new creation," referring to those who have received Christ and His sacrifice on the cross. Christians often talk about becoming new creations when they are born again, but do we truly understand what this means? It's not possible to understand the Holy Spirit or His ministry until we do know this term. You must first understand your identity in Christ in order to understand the Spirit and His role in the new birth. This is the foundation on which our entire relationship with the Holy Spirit is built.

I have met many Christians who seek emotional experiences with the Spirit; I was one of them in my early years of serving the Lord. Over time, it became clear that emotions fade. You may have a powerful encounter with the Spirit one day that affects your emotions, only to feel as if He is nowhere to be found the next day. Unfortunately, living from one emotional experience to the next makes it impossible to have any level of intimacy with the Holy Spirit as He dwells in our born-again spirit. Our relationship with the Spirit is through our inner man which is our born-again spirit. It will require consistent, constant, and focused time given to meditating on the Word of God and fellowshipping with Him each day.

God Looks at the Heart

Saul was the first king of Israel who disobeyed God and lost the kingdom (1 Samuel 15). God sent the prophet Samuel to the house of Jesse in Bethlehem to anoint Saul's successor (1 Samuel 16), inviting Jesse and his sons to come with him to offer a sacrifice to the Lord. Jesse accepted the invitation and brought all but one of his sons, David. The oldest, Eliab, stood out to Samuel among the other sons because of his physical appearance. The prophet thought he had found the new king in Eliab based on what he saw, but God had someone else in mind. Please take note of the Lord's instruction to Samuel about Eliab:

> But the LORD said unto Samuel, Look not on his countenance, or on the height of his stature; because I have refused him: for THE LORD SEETH NOT AS MAN SEETH; for man looketh on the outward appearance, but THE LORD LOOKETH ON THE HEART.
>
> 1 SAMUEL 16:7

This verse is just as relevant for us today as it was for the prophet Samuel. Our connection with God will always be spirit to spirit. God looks at the condition of our hearts, which is why we will never find stability in our Christian journey by relying on our emotions or our five physical senses. Jesus describes four possible conditions of the heart in the parable of the sower which is found in Mark 4:1-20. He described these as the wayside heart, the stony heart, the thorny heart, and the heart that is "good ground."

Society tends to focus on what we can perceive with our physical senses. As a result, we often judge people based on factors such as the color of their skin, body size, or other physical characteristics. The problem with this mindset is that as Christians we tend to follow the path of those around us who are not saved, gravitating toward the natural realm. This results in what Paul refers to as a carnal mindset in Romans 8:5-7:

> For they that are after the flesh do mind the things of the flesh; but THEY THAT ARE AFTER THE SPIRIT THE THINGS OF THE SPIRIT. For to be carnally minded is death; but to be spiritually minded is life and peace. Because the carnal mind is enmity against God: for it is not subject to the law of God, neither indeed can be.

God looks at the heart, not our works. Our attempts to please Him through religious works, such as communion, church attendance, or Bible study, can lead to an unstable Christian life based on self-effort alone. I am not saying these things are not important, but we must examine our motives for pursuing any spiritual discipline. In my experience, far too many Christians pursue such disciplines as religious exercises rather than as measures of outgrowth of our relationship with God. Those who follow this approach in their pursuit of God could be considered carnally minded believers, according to Paul.

The Spiritual Man

I once heard a minister say that we are a spirit, we live in a body, and we have a soul, which is composed of our mind, will, intellect, and emotions. This insight has helped me differentiate between the three parts of my being over the years. I understand that my body is the visible aspect of me, interacting with the world through my five physical senses. While my soul isn't visible, it communicates with me through my emotions. Grasping the concept of the spirit was the most challenging for me.

A natural mirror is designed to reflect what is in front of it. When we look into a mirror, we see a reflection of our physical attributes, such as the color of our hair, eyes, and skin. However, a mirror cannot reflect any characteristics of our inner self. It only showcases our physical body. The condition of our soul, which includes our mind, will, intellect, and emotions, is similarly not reflected in a natural mirror. We don't need a mirror to understand how we feel. Our emotions—like encouragement, discouragement, boldness, or fear—reflect the state of our soul but do not provide insight into the natural or spiritual realms; they only pertain to the soulish realm.

We interact with the physical realm through our five senses and with the soulish realm through our emotions. The spiritual realm, however, is different. While a mirror can indicate if we need to comb our hair, it cannot reveal the condition of our spirit. God has provided us with the Bible, which, according to James 1:22-25, functions like a natural mirror within the spiritual realm. If we wish to understand our spiritual identity, we can open the Bible and read what it says about our spiritual being. The spiritually minded person is a person whose mind is set on the Word of God.

To clarify, while a mirror reflects our physical appearance, it does not show our emotions or the state of our spirit, as both reside in the spiritual realm. We can touch our bodies with our hands and our souls with our words, though we cannot touch our spirits with our hands or words. Our words can cause emotional pain or laughter, which are expressions of the soul, but they can only touch the soul, not the human spirit. God's words, on the other hand, touch the spirit first under the anointing of the Holy Spirit.

The Holy Spirit and the Word of God

The title of this book is *Who Is the Holy Spirit?* In the first chapters, we will delve into understanding the Holy Spirit by first understanding our spiritual nature and the change that occurred inside us when we were born again. Our relationship with the Holy Spirit is spirit to spirit. Without understanding our identity in Christ Jesus through the new birth, we risk having only a superficial relationship with the Spirit.

To understand what is happening in our born-again spirit, we need to investigate the Word of God, realizing the Holy Spirit always works in conjunction with the Word. Developing intimacy with Him requires developing the same level of intimacy with the Word of God, as it forms the foundation of our relationship with Him. Those who pursue the Spirit without also pursuing the Word of God eventually drift off course.

In John 6:63, Jesus told His disciples, "The words that I speak to you are spirit, and they are life" (NKJV), and in John 16:13, Jesus assured them that the Holy Spirit would "guide [them] into all truth" (NKJV). The Holy Spirit always uses the Word of God to guide us into all truth. As mentioned, developing an intimate relationship with the Word of God is inseparable from developing an intimate relationship with the Spirit, and vice versa.

For a more detailed understanding of how the Word of God and the Holy Spirit work together, you can refer to my book, *The Holy Spirit and the Incorruptible Seed.*

Chapter 3

Spirit to Spirit

*It is the spirit that quickeneth; the flesh profiteth nothing: the
words that I speak unto you, they are spirit, and they are life.*

JOHN 6:63

The Word of God and the Holy Spirit are inseparable; they always work hand in hand. God's Word is spiritual, and He reveals things to us through His Word by His Spirit. The Holy Spirit imparts revelation and knowledge into our spirit from the Word to handle life's situations. If we are not aware of our spirit and have not taken time to tune ourselves to the spiritual side of our nature, we will struggle to understand all that has been provided in Christ's redemptive work.

New Creations in Christ Jesus

*Therefore if any man be in Christ, HE IS A NEW CREATURE:
old things are passed away; behold, all things are become new.*

2 CORINTHIANS 5:17

Many preachers often reference 2 Corinthians 5:17 in their messages about salvation. This verse tells us that we have become a "new creature" in the King James Version. Other modern versions use the word "creations." While we frequently discuss being new creations in Christ Jesus, how many of us truly understand what this means? I recall someone who guided me through the prayer of salvation telling me that the Lord had made me new. However, there was no further explanation, and I couldn't see any change in my reflection, which made me question the validity of my experience.

In the second chapter of this book, I introduced you to the three parts of your being: spirit, soul, and physical body. Understanding the concept of being a new creation is crucial for developing a relationship with the Holy Spirit. It's important to realize that we are spirit, soul, and body. When we become a new creation, our spirit is transformed, not our soul or body. God recreates our spirit and gives us a new spiritual nature the moment we make Jesus the Lord of our lives. This spiritual transformation is often referred to as being "born again" by Christians, a new birth from our birth as carnal people.

The new birth does not change our soul or physical being. The term "new creation" refers to the change that occurs in our spirit. In Romans 12:1, Paul tells us that it is our responsibility to "present [our] bodies a living sacrifice" to God. He continues in Romans 12:2, stating that we must be "transformed by the renewing of [our] mind[s]," which pertains to our soul. God will not do this transformation for us. We will explore in detail how to present our bodies and renew our minds.

The New Birth and Your Body and Soul

When we lead people through the prayer of salvation and tell them that everything is new in their life, they might expect instant and dramatic changes to their lives. However, it's important to understand that their physical body does not change when they are born again, as Paul describes in 1 Corinthians 15:53:

For this corruptible must put on incorruption, and this mortal must put on immortality.

He tells us that our body is mortal, still corruptible and has not yet been glorified. For example, I once heard a preacher say, "If you were fat before being saved, you will still be fat afterwards." He was making a point that our bodies did not instantly change when we were born again. Our spirits were recreated, but our bodies were not. Paul tells us in Romans 8:23 that we are still "waiting for…the redemption of our bodies." This will occur at the rapture of the church when every believer receives a glorified body. 1 Corinthians 15:53 refers to this as the corruptible putting on incorruption.

Our souls are also not made new when we receive Jesus as our Lord. Salvation does not change our souls, and they will not change unless we get into the Word of God and allow it to renew our minds (Romans 12:2). We will see that the soul acts as a gateway between our spirit and body, working in alignment with the physical realm until it has been renewed by the Word (James 1:21).

The Lord Is Spirit

Our body and soul were not affected when we were born again. The responsibility for their change has been placed in our hands, as we will discuss in later chapters. For now, it's important to understand that the new birth only caused our spirits to be made new. The Holy Spirit now lives in our spirits, and our relationship with Him will always come through our born-again spirits.

Remember that our bodies and souls are subject to change. We are spiritual beings first and foremost, and the Holy Spirit will help us in this process, but He will not do it for us. As new creations, we are tasked with presenting our physical bodies as a living sacrifice

(Romans 12:1) and renewing our minds with the Word (Romans 12:2). This shows the Holy Spirit wants to manifest His power through us, but this will be delayed until our minds are renewed first spiritually.

In John 4, Jesus had a conversation with a woman from Samaria. He told her, in verse 23, "True worshipers will worship the Father in spirit and truth" (NKJV). God is a spirit, and we relate to Him spirit to spirit. The Holy Spirit is the third person of the Godhead, so we also relate to Him spirit to spirit. Our relationship with Him will always be from our born-again spirit.

The Need to Understand Our Identity in Christ

I have come across many people in the church who know deep down that they belong to Christ. However, most of them only have a basic understanding of this key truth because they lack the profound knowledge of their identity in Christ, which can only come from the Holy Spirit. This is crucial because without understanding your identity in Christ, you won't be able to truly connect with God or develop a close relationship with Him.

Now, can you see why I started this book on the Holy Spirit by discussing the three components of our being? Your connection with the Spirit will remain shallow if you don't understand your identity in Christ or the transformation that took place in your spirit when you were born again; these important factors must take place. The Spirit desires to spend time with us, revealing the understanding of Jesus we will gain as mentioned by Paul in Galatians 1:11-12:

> But I certify you, brethren, that the gospel which was preached of me is not after man. For I neither received it

of man, neither was I taught it, but BY THE REVELA-
TION OF JESUS CHRIST.

Paul tells us that the Gospel he preached came to him "by the
revelation of Jesus Christ." It was the Holy Spirit who imparted this
revelation to him. You will find that the revelation of your identity in
Christ is a part of this revelation, and receiving it will require you to
pursue the Holy Spirit just as Paul did. Everyone who pursues Him
will discover the Spirit and find He is waiting to enter a relationship
with them. It is in this relationship that the Holy Spirit imparts the
"revelation of Jesus Christ."

God Cannot Be Accessed from the Soul or Physical Realm

Jesus told His disciples that religious tradition "makes the word of
God of no effect" (Mark 7:13). Religious tradition does this by drawing our attention away from the spiritual to our self-effort (our works
for God), which originates in the soul and physical part of our being,
referred to as the flesh in the Bible. The flesh is the part of us that
has not yet been redeemed.

Approaching God while feeling depressed, discouraged, angry, or
bitter means you are coming to Him in the flesh rather than in the
spirit. While God will always welcome us, our fleshly desires can create
a barrier between us and Him. Paul teaches in Galatians 5:16-18 that
we can overcome our fleshly desires by learning to walk in the Spirit:

> This I say then, WALK IN THE SPIRIT, AND YE SHALL
> NOT FULFIL THE LUST OF THE FLESH. For the
> flesh lusteth against the Spirit, and the Spirit against the
> flesh: and these are contrary the one to the other: so that

ye cannot do the things that ye would. But if ye be led of
the Spirit, ye are not under the law.

My aim in this book is to show you how to cultivate your relationship with the Holy Spirit. We started by looking at His work in
the new birth of our lives. Many people today are battling with habits or religious traditions that keep them bound to them. There are
various programs, Christian counselors, and support groups available
to help break free from these habits/traditions. I admit I struggled
with many things early in my Christian journey. Perhaps you have
had the same experience as I did, where it was not until I was introduced to the Holy Spirit and began to spend time each day developing my relationship with Him that true freedom was found. He
wants to do the same for you!

Chapter 4

Our Spiritual Mirror

But be ye doers of the word, and not hearers only, deceiving your own selves. For if any be a hearer of the word, and not a doer, he is like unto a man beholding his natural face in a glass: For he beholdeth himself, and goeth his way, and straightway forgetteth what manner of man he was. But whoso looketh into the perfect law of liberty, and continueth therein, he being not a forgetful hearer, but a doer of the work, this man shall be blessed in his deed.

JAMES 1:22-25

The apostle James was a half-brother of Jesus. He compares the Word of God to a natural mirror in James 1:22-25. Paul tells us in 2 Corinthians 5:17 that we have become new creations, referring to what happened in our spirit when we were born again. The Holy Spirit immersed us in Christ (1 Corinthians 12:13) and then sealed us in Christ (Ephesians 1:13) at that moment. We received a new identity based on being sealed into Jesus that cannot be seen with our natural eyes. According to James, the Word acts as a mirror in which we can look and see our new identity in Christ reflected.

The prophet Amos asked how two people can walk together if they do not agree with each other (Amos 3:3). It will be nearly impossible to develop a relationship with the Spirit when viewing ourselves from our natural senses. Coming to agreement with Him requires us to understand our true spiritual identity, as our five physical senses are essentially an inconsistent lens that will not reflect anything but our natural faults and flaws. This is the reason why many Christians view themselves as sinners saved by grace, rather than as new creations who were sinners that were saved by grace.

Sealed in Christ

In whom ye also trusted, after that ye heard the word of truth, the gospel of your salvation: in whom also after that ye believed, YE WERE SEALED with that holy Spirit of promise.

EPHESIANS 1:13

The concept of being "sealed" by the Holy Spirit is essential for understanding our identity in Christ. In Paul's time, seals were used to guarantee that the contents of a package were complete and not defective. A package would only receive a seal after being thoroughly examined to ensure it was intact. If a package was found to be faulty, it would not be sealed.

Senders would pour hot wax onto the flap of an envelope or the string binding a box, then press their insignia into the wax to leave their mark. This marked the package, indicating the sender's identity and guaranteeing delivery.

Paul tells us we "were sealed with that holy Spirit of promise." His readers would have understood this to mean that God examined us after we were born again and found nothing incomplete or defective. When God made us into a new creation, He inspected us and placed His final seal of approval on our hearts. The Holy Spirit baptized us into Christ (1 Corinthians 12:13) when we were born again, resulting in us being sealed in Christ with the Holy Spirit.

You should never view yourself as damaged goods, as many Christians do. Ephesians 4:24 states that we were "created in righteousness and true holiness." This is your new identity. You have been inspected by God and found to be without flaw. God examined you and then sealed you with the Holy Spirit, guaranteeing that you will reach your final destination.

We Have an Identity Crisis

It used to bother me when I read in Scripture that God had accepted me in Christ Jesus (Ephesians 1:6). This was because I was viewing myself through my natural being, looking in the mirror and not seeing anything acceptable. The Holy Spirit helped me see my identity in Christ Jesus and helped me understand that God not only accepted me but also made me acceptable to Him when I was born again. Prior to receiving this revelation, I saw myself as unworthy of being used by Him in any way because of the things I had been taught in church as a child.

There are many people who teach spiritual healing. They focus on the need for our spirits to be healed. I struggled with this concept from the first time I heard a message on the subject. Some of the ministers teaching spiritual healing had international outreaches, so I knew people who gladly followed them and either began teaching spiritual healing or sought people to pray for them to receive healing. After spending many hours searching through Scripture for an answer on spiritual healing, I turned to the Spirit, who led me to 2 Corinthians 5:17, which tells us we are new creations in Christ Jesus. Our spirits do not need to be healed because they have been recreated when we were born again.

We are new creations in Christ Jesus, but what does this mean? Most people I've met over the years have a basic understanding but

lack revelation of their new identity in Christ Jesus. Many saw themselves as mere sinners who had been saved by grace. However, if you
embrace this idea, you will struggle in your Christian journey. The
truth is every Christian was a sinner, was saved by grace, and is a
new creation in Christ Jesus. Our old sinful nature no longer exists.

The Holy Spirit Is Dwelling in You

You may feel inadequate and inferior to be used by God. Many people struggle in this area. However, once you begin to see who you are
in Christ, you will understand how wrong this viewpoint is. Instead
of inferiority, you will see yourself as a conqueror who is superior to
the devil and his antics. The Holy Spirit is standing by to teach you
and lead you through a scriptural journey, which will take you into
the full revelation of your identity in Christ. I have had wonderful
Christians ask me how they can develop a relationship with the Spirit
of God, and I tell them the first step is acknowledging the Spirit of
God dwells in your spirit, which we see clearly in Romans 8:9:

> But ye are not in the flesh, but in the Spirit, if so be that
> THE SPIRIT OF GOD DWELL IN YOU. Now if any
> man have not the Spirit of Christ, he is none of his.

The Holy Spirit lives within the spirit of every Christian who is
born again, as our connection with Him is spiritual. It is vital to understand that we are primarily spiritual beings with souls and physical bodies, acknowledging that the Holy Spirit now dwells within our spirit
when we accept Him. Paul elaborates on this belief in Galatians 4:4-6:

> But when the fulness of the time was come, God sent
> forth his Son, made of a woman, made under the law,

to redeem them that were under the law, that we might receive the adoption of sons. And because ye are sons, God hath sent forth the Spirit of his Son into your hearts, crying, Abba, Father.

If you believe that you are born again and have become a new creature, then you have the Holy Spirit inside you. Paul tells us in Romans 8:11 that the same power that raised Jesus from the dead is within you!

Fully Equipped for the Journey

Having the Holy Spirit within us gives us access to all of God's wisdom, understanding, and faith. Some Christians wish they had the same level of faith as certain ministers; still, they may not realize God has already given them the measure of His faith (Romans 12:3), and the Holy Spirit lives inside them, teaching them how to use the faith they have received in their lives. If you want to learn more about walking by the faith of God or about the measure of His faith you have been given, I have another book called *Walking in the Faith of the Son of God*, which provides you more details about the faith we have received from God.

In Galatians 2:20, Paul tells us that we are to live by the faith of the Son of God. The first step is to start agreeing with what God says, which requires spending dedicated time consistently and constantly focusing on reading His Word (the Bible). As mentioned earlier, the Holy Spirit always works in accordance with the Word. You cannot develop a higher level of intimacy with the Holy Spirit than by reading Scripture and vice versa.

There is a spiritual world we cannot see or discern with our physical senses or emotions, so the only way any of us can look into that realm is through God's Word. James refers to Scripture as a mirror (James 1:22-25) and a window into the spiritual realm. Paul tells us that God has already given us "all spiritual blessings in heavenly places in Christ" (Ephesians 1:3). So, this shows the Word enables us to "see" what has been provided to us from God through Christ's redemptive work.

When you were born again, God put Himself, His life, and His ability in your spirit, and the Holy Spirit brought all of that with Him. Many Christians spend hours looking for more of God because they do not understand He has already given them all of Himself upon salvation. We do not need more of Him but instead must realize that He wants us to surrender to Him. The person fully surrendered to the Spirit of God will have their mind renewed, free of their carnal nature, and their body fully surrendered as the living sacrifice Paul speaks of in Romans 12:1. I believe you are well on your way to joining the ranks of those who have done this and found themselves walking in the victorious Christian life ordained by God for all of His children.

Chapter 5

The Third Baptism

And I will pray the Father, and he shall give you another
Comforter, that he may abide with you for ever; even the
Spirit of truth; whom the world cannot receive, because
it seeth him not, neither knoweth him: but ye know
him; for he dwelleth with you, and shall be in you.

JOHN 14:16-17

In Matthew 10:1, Jesus sent the disciples out to heal the sick and cast out demons. They were able to do these feats with the help of the Holy Spirit, who had been with them but not in them. There is a significant difference between having the Spirit live in our spirits and having His presence come upon us when we are baptized in Him (Acts 1:5).

We have previously touched on the Holy Spirit's activity when a person is born again. In this chapter, our focus will be on baptism with the Spirit. Some ministers and entire denominations may claim that it is impossible to access the Holy Spirit without being baptized with Him, but they are mistaken. Every believer has the Spirit living in their spirit already.

Immersed in Christ by the Spirit

Paul describes the role of the Holy Spirit in salvation in 1 Corinthians 12:13:

> For by one Spirit are we all baptized into one body, whether we be Jews or Gentiles, whether we be bond or free; and have been all made to drink into one Spirit.

Hebrews 6:1-3 gives us a list of foundational doctrines, one of these being the doctrine of baptisms. It's important to note that baptism is listed in the plural here, showing multiple aspects to it. While many Christians focus on water baptism, there is another baptism experience to consider. The first occurs when a person invites Jesus into their heart and is born again. At that moment, they are baptized into the body of Christ by the Spirit (1 Corinthians 12:13). The Holy Spirit is the one who performs this baptism, and it signifies being united with Christ at the point of salvation.

Religion has confused the meaning of baptism, unfortunately. The word *baptism* is translated from a Greek word that literally means to immerse or submerge. The Holy Spirit immerses or submerges our spirit into Jesus and then seals us in Him (Ephesians 1:13), making us a new creation (2 Corinthians 5:17) the moment we confess Jesus as the Lord of our lives and are born again, away from our sinful natures.

John the Baptist told His followers that Jesus would "baptize [them] with the Holy Ghost and with fire" (Luke 3:16). He was not referring to our baptism by the Holy Spirit into Christ or water baptism. The Holy Spirit immerses (baptizes) us in Jesus when we are born again by believing in our hearts and confessing Jesus as our Lord. In water baptism, we are immersed in water to symbolize our baptism by the Spirit at conversion.

Created in Righteousness

And that ye put on the new man, which after
God is created in righteousness and true holiness.

EPHESIANS 4:24

The Holy Spirit baptizes us into Jesus, and we become "new creations" (2 Corinthians 5:17) that are "created in righteousness and true holiness." (Ephesians 4:24). I believe far too many Christians lack a revelation of this fundamental truth.

Paul tells us we have been "made the righteousness of God in him" (2 Corinthians 5:21). The "him" is referring to Jesus. We were baptized into Him by the Spirit (1 Corinthians 12:13) and then sealed into Him (Ephesians 1:13) by the same Holy Spirit. It was at this time we were "created in righteousness and true holiness."

The word translated "made" in 2 Corinthians 5:21 is *ginomai*. It describes a transition from one point to another. You transitioned from a state of unrighteousness to one of righteousness the moment you confessed Jesus as your Lord (Romans 10:9-10). Let's look at Isaiah 54:14 to see the impact a revelation of this can have in your life:

> In righteousness shalt thou be established: thou shalt be
> far from oppression; for thou shalt not fear: and from ter-
> ror; for it shall not come near thee.

I have met many Christians over the years who struggle with feelings of oppression and fear. According to Isaiah, the root cause of this struggle is that they are not established "in righteousness." We were created as righteous and holy the moment we were born again; however, many of us lack the revelation of our true identity.

Baptized by Jesus with the Holy Spirit

After His resurrection, Jesus breathed the Holy Spirit into the disciples' spirits during His first encounter with them (John 20:22); they were born again and received the Holy Spirit into their spirits. However, Jesus told them to wait in Jerusalem "for the promise of the Father" (Acts 1:4) just before His ascension. This reply has led many people to question why they were told to wait for the Holy Spirit when they had already received Him when they were born again. This issue has also caused many to believe there is not a second experience with the Holy Spirit after salvation. However, let's examine this in the context of our discussion on baptisms. First, let's look at Jesus' full statement in Acts 1:4-5:

> And, being assembled together with them, commanded them that they should not depart from Jerusalem, but wait for the promise of the Father, which, saith he, ye have heard of me. For John truly baptized with water; but YE SHALL BE BAPTIZED WITH THE HOLY GHOST not many days hence.

In these verses, Jesus talks about a third baptism in which He will immerse the disciples in the Holy Spirit, also known today as the baptism in the Spirit. The first baptism refers to the Holy Spirit immersing us in Christ (accepting Christ into our hearts), which is followed by water baptism, performed by a person, which serves as an outward expression of our first baptism. Finally, Jesus baptizes (immerses) us in the Holy Spirit which is the experience He referenced in Acts 1:5.

Conflicting interpretations of John 20 and Acts 1 arise because people often do not consider these three different baptisms. In later chapters, I will discuss the third baptism in more detail and its significance in developing a relationship with the Holy Spirit and working in His anointing. Some may experience this as part of their conversion of faith when they confess Jesus as their Lord and are born again. In contrast, others may receive it as a separate experience that happens away from the moment of their conversion to Christ. For now, it's important to understand the need for every Christian to be baptized with the Spirit.

Chapter 6

The Guarantee of
Our Full Redemption

*And that ye put on the new man, which after God
is created in righteousness and true holiness.*

EPHESIANS 4:24

Many Christians often find themselves stuck in a cycle where they feel like the enemy, the devil, is overcoming them. While they believe in God and want to fulfill His plan, they struggle to understand what it is or how to find it. Most focus more on the physical world rather than the spiritual realm, knowing that God is a spirit but lacking a deeper understanding of the spiritual realm and their own spiritual nature.

Developing a relationship with the Holy Spirit requires first recognizing the existence of the spiritual realm. The spiritual created the natural realm. I've personally found the Spirit's guidance to become clearer as I become more in tune with the spiritual realm, and I believe you will find the same to be true for you.

The Natural and Spiritual Realms

In Ephesians 1:3, Paul tells us God has blessed us with all spiritual blessings, which are stored up for us in the spiritual realm. God has given us the responsibility to bring these blessings into the natural realm and sent the Holy Spirit to teach us how to do this and to guide us in our journey.

When my relationship with God seems to become more difficult, it's helpful to take inventory of how I have been spending my time. In most cases, this exercise reveals that my focus has drifted away from the Word of God and the time that should have been spent sitting with Him.

You may find the same in your life if you take an inventory of how your time is spent each day. The more we move away from the Word of God to other things, the less we will be in tune with the Holy Spirit. This doesn't necessarily mean we are sinning, as maybe we may have been spending more time watching news programs, television shows, or movies. While these activities are not necessarily sinful, they can cause us to focus more on the natural realm (the world) and less on the spiritual realm (God).

As He Is, so Are We in This World

Paul exhorts us to "put on the new man," which was created in "righteousness and true holiness" (Ephesians 4:24). I have spent a lot of time over the years meditating on this verse. It did not make sense in the early years of my Christian journey because I lacked revelation of the three parts of my being: body, soul, and spirit. The church I was saved in taught a progressive holiness, which basically meant we become more holy over time. My mind could not grasp how I could have been made righteous and holy but still needed to progressively become more holy as the church I grew up in taught. Another

Scripture that I struggled with, which complements Ephesians 4:24, is 1 John 4:17:

> Herein is our love made perfect, that we may have boldness in the day of judgment: because AS HE IS, SO ARE WE IN THIS WORLD.

John tells us we are identical to Jesus "in this world." This is a radical statement and challenged my belief system when I first saw it. I would look in the mirror, read the verse, and then look again. What I saw reflected did not look like Jesus! It just did not seem possible I was identical to Jesus and took years for me to receive revelation from the Spirit to what this Scripture was referring.

If you think about it logically, Jesus was able to appear and disappear in a room with locked doors and windows after His resurrection. Can you or I do this? The answer, of course, is no, we can't. Our physical body has not yet been glorified for this ability, which we see in Ephesians 1:13-14:

> In whom ye also trusted, after that ye heard the word of truth, the gospel of your salvation: in whom also after that ye believed, ye were sealed with that holy Spirit of promise, which is the earnest of our inheritance until the redemption of the purchased possession, unto the praise of his glory.

Our spirits have been recreated, and they are the part of our being John spoke of in 1 John 4:17. Our souls are renewed with the Word of God, but our bodies will not be redeemed until Christ returns and we receive our glorified bodies; the Holy Spirit was sent as the guarantee of this. Our confidence in the Lord's soon return and glorification of our physical bodies and souls will grow as our relationship with the Holy Spirit grows.

Waiting for Our Full Redemption

So, our bodies were bought with the blood of Christ, but they have not yet been redeemed. Paul tells us the Holy Spirit was sent as our guarantee so that we will not be left here on our own, as mentioned in the paragraph before. Christ will return, and our bodies will be redeemed. We see similar wording in Romans 8:23:

> And not only they, but ourselves also, which have the firstfruits of the Spirit, even we ourselves groan within ourselves, waiting for the adoption, to wit, the redemption of our body.

Our bodies have been bought by the blood of Jesus, so we are currently waiting for His return and the full redemption of our bodies. The Holy Spirit helped me understand His role as our guarantee of this using green stamps my mom used to collect when I was growing up.

The grocery store we shopped at would issue a certain number of green stamps for every dollar spent, which my mom would place in a drawer at our house. She would receive a catalog of items each month that held a list of things that could be bought with the stamps. There were items for the house my mom was interested in, but there were also toys and things that I wanted. My mom would sometimes give me those stamps, so I could redeemed them for a toy or whatever else I wanted at the store. This is the same way it is with our bodies; Jesus paid the necessary price to redeem us so we can be the Christians we want to be with Him.

You are a spirit, have a soul, and live in a body. Christ has bought all three parts of our being, but our souls and bodies have not yet been redeemed; we are still waiting for this. The Holy Spirit has taken up residence in our spirits and provides us the guarantee that Jesus will return, and we will receive glorified bodies.

Chapter 7

Exchanging the Corruptible for the Incorruptible

Behold, I shew you a mystery; We shall not all sleep, but we shall
all be changed, in a moment, in the twinkling of an eye, at
the last trump: for the trumpet shall sound, and the dead shall
be raised incorruptible, and we shall be changed. FOR THIS
CORRUPTIBLE MUST PUT ON INCORRUPTION, AND
THIS MORTAL MUST PUT ON IMMORTALITY. So when
this corruptible shall have put on incorruption, and this mortal
shall have put on immortality, then shall be brought to pass
the saying that is written, Death is swallowed up in victory.

1 CORINTHIANS 15:51-54

Y ou have been bought, spirit, soul, and body, with the most precious thing God has–the blood of Jesus. We saw in the last chapter our souls and bodies have not yet been redeemed, even though our spirits have. Paul tells us in 1 Corinthians 15:53 the "corruptible must put on incorruption." He was referring to the full redemption of our bodies, which will happen when Jesus returns for His true church.

I referred to 1 John 4:17 in chapter 5, which tells us we are identical to Jesus in this world. By process of elimination, the Scriptures we've looked at in Ephesians 1, Romans 8, and 1 Corinthians 15 tell us he could not be talking about our physical bodies that have not yet been redeemed. Scriptures like 1 Corinthians 13:9-10 show us that John also could not have been talking about our souls either, which we have already said consist of our minds, wills, intellects, and emotions:

> For we know in part, and we prophesy in part. But when
> that which is perfect is come, then that which is in part
> shall be done away.

Our natural knowledge is limited. The Holy Spirit knows everything about every subject imaginable. His knowledge is limitless. He has taught me so many things that it is hard to recount them all. His ability to do so, though, is limited by our willingness to allow Him to help, as some may not want His help as they should. I have found Him more than willing to help me at work, in my relationships with friends and family, and in ministry.

The Mind of Christ

There are two verses that come to mind when I think of how the Holy Spirit has helped me over the years:

> *For who hath known the mind of the Lord, that he may*
> *instruct him? but we have the mind of Christ.*
>
> 1 CORINTHIANS 2:16

> *But ye have an unction from the Holy One,*
> *and ye know all things.*
>
> 1 JOHN 2:20

Like 1 John 4:17, it is impossible to understand what these verses tell us without considering the three parts of our being—spirit, soul, and body. We do not "know all things" in our natural brains; in our spirits, though, we have the perfect wisdom and knowledge of God through the Holy Spirit, who was sent to teach and reveal God's divine wisdom and knowledge to us.

So, from the things we've looked at in the last chapter and in this one, we see it is our born- again spirits that are identical to Jesus in this world. Our spirits at this moment are recreated and exactly like Jesus is! This is a vital truth missed by many Christians, which is why so many struggle in their pursuit of God. They view themselves as sinners striving to become acceptable to God instead of new creations that are identical to Christ who were made righteous and holy (Ephesians 4:24) when they were born again.

Immersed and Sealed
in Christ by the Spirit

The things we have looked at in this book are completely different from what is taught in most churches today. You are not a sinner saved by grace, a phrase commonly heard in churches today. The truth is we were sinners and were saved by grace, but we are identical to Christ (1 John 4:17) and have been made righteous and holy (Ephesians 4:24). Can you see the difference?

This book is titled *Who Is the Holy Spirit,* and as I said in chapter 1, it may seem as if we have gone on another track with this book's direction. The truth though is we have not. There are many books available that focus on the Spirit and jump right in without laying any groundwork for readers. I felt the Holy Spirit direct me to begin with a study of the three parts of our being because you cannot experience any level of intimacy with Him viewing yourself as a sinner saved by grace.

There are people who will accuse you of joining a cult for saying you are identical to Jesus. For clarification, I am not saying we became God when we were born again, which is something often claimed by cults. We are not God, but our spirits have been fully redeemed and are identical to Jesus today because of salvation. When a person accepts Jesus as their Lord and Savior, the Holy Spirit immerses them into Jesus (1 Corinthians 12:13) and then seals them in Christ with Himself (Ephesians 1:13).

We put on "immortality" (1 Corinthians 15:53) when we are born again, baptized into Jesus by the Spirit, and then are sealed in Christ with the Spirit. There will still be problems in our flesh, and our minds will still need to be renewed by the Word of God daily, but our spirits become new creations in Christ Jesus and are now just like Jesus in this world.

Some people interpret 1 John 4:17 as saying we will be like Jesus one day. If this is true, why does John tell us we are like Jesus in this world? The truth is we are identical to Jesus and can renew our minds and walk in the fullness of all God has planned for our lives. We can begin to experience heaven here on earth, but only to the degree we renew our minds and develop our relationship with the Holy Spirit.

You Can Experience a Taste of Heaven in This World

Jesus taught His disciples a prayer that we commonly refer to as the Lord's prayer, found in Matthew 6:9-13:

> In this manner, therefore, pray:
> Our Father in heaven,
> Hallowed be Your name.
> Your kingdom come.

Your will be done
On earth as it is in heaven.
Give us this day our daily bread.
And forgive us our debts,
As we forgive our debtors.
And do not lead us into temptation,
But deliver us from the evil one.
For Yours is the kingdom, power, and glory forever.
Amen. (NKJV)

Our spirits are as perfect and complete as they will be the day we leave this world. One-third of our salvation is complete when God places heaven in the spirit of every born-again believer. You can experience it to the degree you renew your mind. It is the renewing of our minds, in conjunction with our willingness to submit to the Holy Spirit, which will enable us to experience a manifestation of what is in our spirits in our physical bodies.

Romans 8:9 tells us if "anyone does not have the Spirit of Christ, he is not His" (NKJV). You cannot be born again and not have the Holy Spirit. He dwells in our spirits only because they have been recreated in "righteousness and true holiness" (Ephesians 4:24). It is because we have been born again and made to be identical to Jesus (1 John 4:17) that the Spirit is able to inhabit our spirits.

Proverbs 23:7 tells us, "For as he thinks in his heart, so is he" (NKJV). Salvation is complete in our spirits, but our ability to benefit from it is affected by our thinking. We have access to all of God's provision, but our ignorance about the change our spirits underwent in the new birth prohibits us from accessing it. As I've mentioned several times in this chapter, your spirit is identical to Jesus, but it is not becoming like Him. You are as righteous and holy today as you will be when you enter heaven.

Your spirit is completely saved today. I imagine some of you might read this and wonder how that helps you go about your daily life. The Bible tells us in Proverbs 23:7 that our life moves in the direction of our dominant thought. If you limit yourself by viewing yourself as only human or as the victim of circumstances, you will not experience the power of God that is already in your born-again spirit. If, on the other hand, you begin to think about who you are in Christ and begin to think about your identity in Christ Jesus, you will start to release the life of God that is in your spirit. The Holy Spirit is standing by to help you. Lean on Him and let Him guide you into total victory.

Chapter 8

One Spirit with the Lord

But he that is joined unto the Lord is one spirit.

1 CORINTHIANS 6:17

Paul tells us we have been joined to the Lord. According to the Strong's Greek dictionary, the word translated "joined" literally means to be glued together. We have already looked at 1 John 4:17, which tells us we are identical to Jesus in this world now and that it was speaking of our born-again spirits. We are one with Him because our spirit has been joined, or glued together, with His Spirit.

I've heard Christians discuss the importance of following the Spirit of God. While it is true that we should follow Him, how many of us have taken the time to really consider what this means? Paul tells us in Romans 8:14 that the children of God are to be led by the Spirit. This verse illustrates a picture of us living in complete dependence on the Holy Spirit. Therefore, following the Spirit of God requires us to first depend on Him, which in turn necessitates acknowledging His presence in our lives.

Put On the New Man

Understanding the Holy Spirit requires us to first understand our spiritual nature as born-again Christians. We are joined to the Lord and become one spirit with Him. The *Vine's Expository Dictionary* (1985) tells us the word translated "one" literally means a singular one to the exclusion of another, depicting a position of literally being united in purpose.

If you are truly born again, you have received a new spirit, been "glued" together with Jesus, and united in purpose with Him in your spirit. Our spirits are not just like Him, as they have been recreated (2 Corinthians 5:17). Your old sinful nature no longer exists, and every barrier between you and God has been removed.

Paul reminds us in Ephesians 4:24 we can "put on the new man which was created according to God, in true righteousness and holiness" (NKJV), which he was talking about our spiritual man. The translated words "put on" portray an act similar to what we do when getting dressed in clothes. Our spirits have been recreated, but this change will not affect our lives if we do not gain a revelation of our spiritual identity and clothe ourselves in it.

I have met many Christians who struggle in their relationship with the Holy Spirit. They know He exists but lack any understanding of Him or the relationship He wants. In my experience, the number one reason for lack of knowledge is a sense of unworthiness to fellowship with God, stemming from our misunderstanding of what happened when we were born again.

Your Old Spiritual Man Is Dead

Religious teachings have led to a gross misunderstanding of our spiritual nature. Many Christians think they received a new spirit but still have their old one that is dead in trespasses and sin. I have heard ministers teach the Spirit of Christ entered our spirits when we were born again with the nature of God, describing a position of having a dual spirit—one with the sinful nature and a second with God's nature in it.

Without realizing it, those who embrace this belief depict Christians as living in a condition of spiritual schizophrenia. With two spirits, we are described as spiritual Dr. Jekyll and Mr. Hyde! You need to understand this is not what the Bible teaches. Notice the words of Paul in Romans 6:1-11:

> What shall we say then? Shall we continue in sin, that grace may abound? God forbid. How shall we, that are dead to sin, live any longer therein? Know ye not, that so many of us as were baptized into Jesus Christ were baptized into his death? Therefore we are buried with him by baptism into death: that like as Christ was raised up from the dead by the glory of the Father, even so we also should walk in newness of life. For if we have been planted together in the likeness of his death, we shall be also in the likeness of his resurrection: knowing this, that our old man is crucified with him, that the body of sin might be destroyed, that henceforth we should not serve sin. For he that is dead is freed from sin. Now if we be dead with Christ, we believe that we shall also live with him: knowing that Christ being raised from the dead dieth no more; death hath no more dominion over him. For in that he died, he died unto sin once: but in that he liveth, he liveth unto God. Likewise reckon ye also yourselves to be dead indeed unto sin, but alive unto God through Jesus Christ our Lord.

In these verses, we understand that our old self is dead and gone. It was associated with "the body of sin," which refers to the sinful nature we all inherited from the transgression of Adam and Eve. I've encountered Christians who believe that their old self is resurrected every day and needs to be put to death, leading them to seek God's forgiveness as if they are approaching Him for the first time. This belief is incorrect. Your old self died the moment you believed in your heart and confessed Jesus as your Lord. At that moment, your new self was created.

Previously, you were compelled to sin by the sinful nature of your old self, but that nature is now gone. Your spirit has been recreated, and you possess a new nature that compels you to be righteous. The Holy Spirit lives within your new spirit and is always available to help you in your life. For Him to assist you, you must acknowledge the work that has been completed in your spirit and recognize that He is with you in your soul. This acknowledgment will be easier to receive if you spend time each day in communion with Him.

Why Do We Sin?

Your old sinful nature was crucified with Christ, buried with Him, and you have been spiritually resurrected with a brand-new, sinless nature. The old sinful nature created a barrier between you and God that has now been eliminated. It is because of this change that you can develop a relationship with the Holy Spirit and spend time fellowshipping with Him each day (2 Corinthians 13:14).

I can sense there will be people reading this book who will question the things I'm saying in this chapter. If our old nature was the thing that caused us to sin, why do so many of us struggle with sin today? The most often quoted Scripture I've heard people use as "proof" to counter our new nature is Romans 7:18-20:

> For I know that in me (that is, in my flesh,) dwelleth no good thing: for to will is present with me; but how to perform that which is good I find not. For the good that

I would I do not: but the evil which I would not, that I
do. Now if I do that I would not, it is no more I that do
it, but sin that dwelleth in me.

Many Bible teachers quote these verses to describe the struggles
they say we all face in our Christian journey, even after repentance.
The problem with their argument is Paul was not speaking of what
his life really was. In context, these verses describe a person who is
trying to please God out of self-effort, the person who tries to earn
God's favor instead of just standing in His grace and appropriating
everything He has provided by faith.

If you try and work to please God through self-effort, you will
find yourself struggling with the issues Paul describes in Romans 7.
Jesus had to go to the cross because it is impossible for us to please
God in our own merits. I previously mentioned Romans 8:14 as an
answer, which tells us children of God should be led by the Spirit of
God, and said the verse describes a person completely dependent on
the Holy Spirit. It is literally impossible to live in our human ability
and please God so we must depend on Him to lead us in every step
of our Christian journey.

Entering into the
Victorious Christian Life

The point Paul was trying to make in Romans 7 is that we cannot
succeed in our Christian journey without the help of the Holy Spirit.
We must come to a place of complete dependence on Him if our
goal is to live in the supernatural ability of God already present in
our born-again spirits. Paul is not telling us we will have to struggle
continually to please God even after being saved. Notice his closing
statement in Romans 7:24-26:

O wretched man that I am! who shall deliver me from
the body of this death? I thank God through Jesus Christ
our Lord. So then with the mind I myself serve the law
of God; but with the flesh the law of sin.

It is only through Christ Jesus any person can be born again. His
death, burial, and resurrection opened the door for us to be born
again, be joined to Him, and become one spirit. Paul argues the case
that it is impossible for any person to approach God or please Him
in their own strength. He follows this chapter with Romans 8, which
provides us a comparison of the life lived from the flesh and the one
lived after "the things of the Spirit" (Romans 8:5).

The word *spirit* is used only once in Romans 7. In this chapter,
Paul shows us the futility of a life lived independent of God. We all
want to live a life that is pleasing to Him but cannot do so outside of
our position in Christ. Romans 8 provides a totally different picture,
where the word *spirit* is mentioned twenty-one times. Paul uses the
word *spirit* to show the power of living from our born-again spirits
a life completely dependent on the Spirit of God.

Chapter 9

Learning to Depend on the Spirit

For as many as are led by the Spirit of God,
they are the sons of God.

ROMANS 8:14

S ons and daughters of God can and must be led by the Spirit
of God in every area of their lives. Doing so requires us to first
understand our inability to live without Him, as mentioned earlier.
We have new spirits and all God's abilities in our born-again spirits, and every Christian is ordained by God to experience victory in
all areas of life. I believe it is our lack of revelation about the change
that took place in our spirits when we were born again that hinders
our faith moving forward.

The Spirit-led life is a life lived in complete dependence on the
Holy Spirit, lived from the new spirit in which He resides. I believe
this is the life Paul describes in Galatians 2:20:

> I am crucified with Christ: nevertheless I live; yet not I,
> but Christ liveth in me: and the life which I now live in
> the flesh I live by the faith of the Son of God, who loved
> me, and gave himself for me.

Everything we have looked at up to this point is foundational revelation to our being able to develop a relationship with the Holy Spirit. Our spirits have been born again, and He has taken up residence within us. However, there is still a barrier we must overcome to enter into the Spirit-led life fully, which is our flesh.

We Are Dead to Sin

Romans 6:11-13 offers some insight into the influence of our flesh in our lives:

> Likewise reckon ye also yourselves to be dead indeed unto sin, but alive unto God through Jesus Christ our Lord. Let not sin therefore reign in your mortal body, that ye should obey it in the lusts thereof. Neither yield ye your members as instruments of unrighteousness unto sin: but yield yourselves unto God, as those that are alive from the dead, and your members as instruments of righteousness unto God.

You are dead to sin but still have the flesh to deal with. I once heard a minister compare this understanding to a corpse. A dead body is lifeless, but people working in morgues have reported they will sometimes see things like a corpse sitting up or an arm moving. This happens because of electrical impulses in the body that last for a while.

Like a dead corpse in a coffin, our sin nature is dead. Just as a human corpse will sometimes have electrical impulses that cause it to do things like having the eyes open or a finger twitch, our flesh nature will sometimes act up, causing us to do things we know are contrary to God. Many times, this is a result of our spending more time at worldly things, such as sporting events, news broadcasts, or movies, than in fellowship with the Holy Spirit.

Strongholds in the Soul

Our old, sinful man is dead, buried with Christ, and we have been spiritually born again, no longer having a sin nature driving us to sin. There is no boundary on God's side keeping us from entering into a relationship with the Holy Spirit. You will find the Holy Spirit desires you to have direct access to His presence. In fact, God's best is for you to go directly to the Holy Spirit, not people, for help.

Notice, in the paragraph before, I said there are no boundaries on God's side that keep us from entering fellowship with the Spirit. Paul speaks of boundaries that we allow to be built within us in 2 Corinthians 10:3-5:

> For though we walk in the flesh, we do not war after the flesh: (for the weapons of our warfare are not carnal, but mighty through God to the pulling down of strong holds;) casting down imaginations, and every high thing that exalteth itself against the knowledge of God, and bringing into captivity every thought to the obedience of Christ.

If you are born again, the sin nature that used to drive you to sin is gone. In these verses, Paul tells us the barriers that cause us to struggle in our relationship with God are strongholds consisting of "arguments and every high thing that exalts itself against the knowledge of God" (2 Corinthians 10:5, NKJV). This is mainly speaking of thought patterns. Although many people think strongholds are demonic holds over things like cities or nations, they are wrong. Biblically, strongholds are always thought patterns we have allowed to be built in our souls that are not in line with the Word of God.

Sin and Our Selfish Desires

For if we have been planted together in the likeness of his death, we
shall be also in the likeness of his resurrection: knowing this, that
our old man is crucified with him, THAT THE BODY OF SIN
MIGHT BE DESTROYED, that henceforth we should not serve sin.

ROMANS 6:5-6

Notice Paul's reference to the *body of sin*, telling us it has been done *away with,* so why does it seem we still struggle with it? Understanding this reference requires an understanding of the word *sin* translated in this verse. It always refers to the type of sin that always originates in self-effort or selfish desires.

There are many ways to describe the body of sin. For a Christian, it is mainly speaking of thought patterns built in our souls that push us to do things that are not pleasing to God. This pattern first started to become clear to me one day while meditating on Romans 1:18-19:

> For the wrath of God is revealed from heaven against
> all ungodliness and unrighteousness of men, who hold
> the truth in unrighteousness; because that which may be
> known of God is manifest in them; for God hath shewed
> it unto them.

In these verses, we encounter three important terms relevant to our discussion: wrath, ungodliness, and unrighteousness. God's wrath reflects His internal disposition to oppose any person or action that contradicts His nature. The term "ungodliness" refers to actions derived from a mindset that lacks reverence for God. Meanwhile, "unrighteousness" describes a person who behaves in ways that are contrary to God's righteousness and the revelation they have received. It is crucial for us to understand these terms and their proper definitions, as they have often been misused by religious traditions to condemn many Christians throughout church history. Grasping their true meaning will help you avoid falling into this trap.

Finding the Spirit in Christ's Redemptive Work

I have met many wonderful people over the years who struggle in developing a relationship with the Holy Spirit. When He directed me to write this book, I thought it would be more focused on the Spirit and His ministry. He has shown me, though, as I've been writing that it is impossible to understand the Holy Spirit without first understanding our identity in Christ.

We have been looking at strongholds in our soul that cause us to act in ways contrary to our new spiritual nature. It is these strongholds that cause barriers between us and the Holy Spirit. Though He will not remove them for us, the Holy Spirit will help us if we commit ourselves to spend time every day meditating in the Word of God and then sitting with Him. One of the most profound truths He has shown me is revelation of the plan of God arises from our spirits during times of fellowship with Him and reason rises from our souls during times of fellowship with the carnal world and self-effort.

Paul tells us in Ephesians 2:3 that we were once children of wrath—past tense; this was our nature before we made Jesus the Lord of our lives. Our spiritual nature has now changed due to the new birth, and we are children of righteousness now. The spirit within us was dead in trespasses and sin but now has been recreated and is alive in righteousness and holiness as a result. Just as our old spirit taught us how to sin, our new spirit will teach us to walk in righteousness if we allow it to.

Many Christians have complained to me about the struggles they have with their flesh. This is because they are more in tune with their outer man than the new spirit within them. You may be in the same place; it is where I found myself stuck until the Holy Spirit helped me break free from the strongholds. He did this by revealing my identity in Christ to me. My relationship with the Spirit developed almost effortlessly in line with the growth of this revelation of my identity, and I believe yours will too as you grow in the revelation of who you are in Christ Jesus.

IDENTITY REVEALED BY THE SPIRIT

If ye then be risen with Christ, seek those things which are above, where Christ sitteth on the right hand of God. Set your affection on things above, not on things on the earth. For ye are dead, and your life is hid with Christ in God. When Christ, who is our life, shall appear, then shall ye also appear with him in glory.

COLOSSIANS 3:1-4

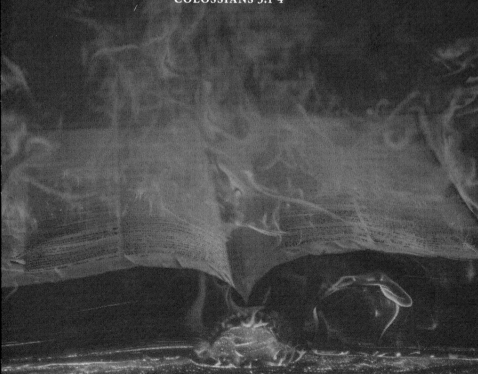

Chapter 10

You Are Righteous and Holy

But ye have not so learned Christ; if so be that ye have heard
him, and have been taught by him, as the truth is in Jesus: that
ye put off concerning the former conversation the old man, which
is corrupt according to the deceitful lusts; and be renewed in the
spirit of your mind; and that ye put on the new man, which
after God is created in righteousness and true holiness.

EPHESIANS 4:20-24

I was first introduced to the Holy Spirit in an emotional encounter that lasted for more than four hours, occurring in the winter of 1991 in my second year of Bible school. The Spirit introduced Himself to me in a way that absolutely changed my life forever. This experience introduced me to an emotional connection with God that could not be kept over a prolonged period of time. I found myself feeling close to Him one day and then completely separated the next. In a very real sense, I began to act like an addict running from meeting to meeting seeking experiences with God that would give me an emotional high.

The Word Is Always First

I enjoy spending time with the Holy Spirit but am not dependent on my emotions or physical senses to do so as He always works in line with the written Word of God. One of the first Scriptures the Spirit led me to as I struggled to hang on to the emotional high experienced when I first met Him was Psalm 119:11:

> Thy word have I hid in mine heart, that I might not sin
> against thee.

I have already shared in earlier chapters that we are a three-part being: spirit, soul, and body. It is our spirit that has already changed, as Ephesians 4:24 tells us our spirits were "created according to God, in true righteousness and holiness" (NKJV). This happened when we were born again, receiving a brand-new spirit that is as righteous and holy today as it will be the day we enter into heaven. The Holy Spirit will use the Word to reveal your spiritual identity, where you are glued together with Christ. He took me to Psalm 119:11 and showed me it would be impossible to develop any level of intimacy with Him without first developing an intimate relationship with the Word of God.

We Are "in" Christ Jesus

Notice once again the previously mentioned verse of 2 Corinthians 5:17:

> Therefore if any man be in Christ, he is a new creature: old
> things are passed away; behold, all things are become new.

The word translated "in" displays a condition in which something operates from the inside of something else. We see in 1 Corinthians 12:13 the Holy Spirit baptized us into the body of Christ when we were born again. He immersed us in Jesus and then sealed us in Christ with Himself (Ephesians 1:13).

Your spirit was recreated and sealed in Christ, as the old, sinful spirit is buried and no longer exists. You will never understand the Holy Spirit without first understanding this truth. I have met several Christians who struggle in their Christian journey just as I did in the early years with their spiritual identity. In most cases, they have no revelation of the change that occurred in their spirit when they were born again or of the impact on their life from being sealed in Christ.

It was not your physical body or soul that was changed when you were born again but your spirit. We do not teach these things in church, and many people have given up when they did not experience an immediate change in their emotional or physical being upon being saved. They thought everything would change at once and all their problems would go away.

Your physical body should reflect the presence and the work of God in your life; it is only as you renew your mind (Romans 12:2) with His Word that it will do so though. We are encouraged to "put on the new man which was created according to God, in true righteousness and holiness" (NKJV), but the choice to do so is ours alone to make. The Holy Spirit was sent to help us do this, but He will not force us to do so.

We Are Righteous in This World

Your spirit was recreated and is as righteous and holy today as when you leave this life and enter heaven. Unfortunately, this is not a truth that is widely known due to a lack of correct teaching in our churches about the new birth and the change our spirits undergo when we were born again. The result of this lack of knowledge is many Christians work and work to become righteous. They exhaust themselves trying to earn what they already are because of sitting in churches, week after week, who preach religious traditions and denominational doctrines instead of the true Gospel of Jesus Christ.

If you are a Christian, God has recreated your spirit, and it is righteous and holy. You cannot become more righteous or more holy, so it is, therefore, not a matter of becoming more righteous but instead it is a matter of learning to release the righteousness already in your spirit. The Holy Spirit was sent to teach us and will lead us into revelation knowledge of this foundational truth if we will let Him.

I have already referenced 1 John 4:17, but let's take a look at it again:

> Herein is our love made perfect, that we may have boldness in the day of judgment: because as he is, so are we in this world.

The only way to understand this verse is to see it speaking of our born-again spirits. The transformation took place within us. It is only because we have been recreated, and are righteous and holy, that the Holy Spirit was able to enter our spirits and remain there.

Victory Follows Mind Renewal

Your salvation is already complete in your spirit. When you made Jesus the Lord of your life, you spirit was as saved as it will ever be. Your spirit is not being saved, and it does not need to be healed as those who teach spiritual healing claim because it is righteous and holy. The Holy Spirit cannot intermingle with unrighteousness and so could not have taken up residence in our spirits if this were not true.

Your spirit is already complete. So, our minds need to be renewed today (Romans 12:2) to walk in the fullness of all that has been provided to us through Christ's redemptive work and develop an intimate relationship with the Holy Spirit. I believe this is what James was speaking of in James 1:21:

> Wherefore lay apart all filthiness and superfluity of naugh-
> tiness, and receive with meekness the engrafted word,
> which is able to save your souls.

We see in this verse above that it is the "implanted Word" that "is able to save our souls." The word translated "implanted" describes something that has been brought into a living union similar to a suc-cessfully engrafted shoot that has been permanently fixed in the soil. We see in the parable of the sower (Mark 4:1-20) the soil in which God's Word is planted is our soul. The truly victorious life we all desire is found in learning to renew our minds to the truth of our identity in Christ Jesus. We see in John 14:26 it is the Holy Spirit who was sent to reveal Jesus to us:

> But the Comforter, which is the Holy Ghost, whom the
> Father will send in my name, he shall teach you all things,
> and bring all things to your remembrance, whatsoever I
> have said unto you.

You will never receive anything from the Holy Spirit that did not come from Jesus. God sent the Holy Spirit to teach us and reveal Jesus to us; the Spirit does this through the written Word. If we are not spending time each day meditating on Scripture, the Holy Spirit cannot impart revelation knowledge to us. This knowledge is how our minds become renewed by the Word of God.

Chapter 11

Sealed with the Spirit

In whom ye also trusted, after that ye heard the word of
truth, the gospel of your salvation: in whom also after that
ye believed, ye were sealed with that holy Spirit of promise,
which is the earnest of our inheritance until the redemption
of the purchased possession, unto the praise of his glory.

EPHESIANS 1:13-14

Y ou were sealed in Christ with the Holy Spirit after you "heard the word of truth, the gospel of your salvation," as the verse above states. There are different types of seals, but the type of seal Paul refers to is one used on official documents to confirm authenticity of a document. These seals were used when Paul wrote Ephesians on official documents. They consisted of an imprint made by a signet ring in wax used to seal the document.

A seal can be used to verify authenticity, but it can also be used as a preservative. An example of this is when people can preserves: they put the food in a jar that is airtight, place the lid on the jar, and then seal it with something like paraffin. This creates an airtight seal that will keep impurities from getting into the jar and also keep the preserves fresh.

Vacuum-Packed with the Spirit

We have already looked at Ephesians 4:24 and understood our spirit was recreated at the moment of salvation in "righteousness and holiness," and also seen in 1 John 4:17 that we are identical to Jesus in this world. The first few paragraphs of this chapter introduced the concept of sealing something to keep it fresh. Notice Paul's description of how this applies to us in 1 Corinthians 6:17:

> But he that is joined unto the Lord is one spirit.

We have been sealed in Jesus with the Holy Spirit and have become one spirit with Him. This is an amazing statement that requires the Spirit's help for us to grasp. If you have made Jesus the Lord of your life, you are literally vacuum-packed and sealed with the Holy Spirit. The Spirit of God has been placed in our spirits and together, Paul tells us we are crying out, "Abba, Father" (Galatians 4:6).

Jesus' Righteousness, Sanctification, and Redemption Is Ours

I have heard many Christians quote Isaiah 64:6 to describe the perception they have of themselves and their standing with God:

> But we are all as an unclean thing, and all our righteousnesses are as filthy rags; and we all do fade as a leaf; and our iniquities, like the wind, have taken us away.

This verse is often used to support the religious argument that we are not identical to Jesus as 1 John 4:17 tells us. The problem with this train of thought is it does not take into consideration the fact that Isaiah 64:6 was written before the cross. When I am confronted with this belief, I have found the best thing to do is point people to 1 Corinthians 1:30:

> But of him are ye in Christ Jesus, who of God is made unto us wisdom, and righteousness, and sanctification, and redemption.

Isaiah lived before Jesus was "made unto us wisdom, and righteousness, and sanctification, and redemption." People living under the Old Covenant could not be born again as we are today, so they served God but kept their spiritually dead spirits. The cross was in their future and is in our past.

It was true people living during Isaiah's day had a level of righteousness that was no different from a filthy rag because they were spiritually dead. We have been born again, and we have received a new spirit that is just as righteous and holy as Jesus is. Our righteousness is Jesus' righteousness, and any person claiming their righteousness is like a filthy rag is essentially calling the Lord a filthy rag.

Your Spirit Is Pure

Jesus has been "made unto us wisdom, and righteousness, and sanctification, and redemption." The word that is translated "made" in this verse is *ginomai*, standing for a transition from one condition to another, resulting in a fundamental change to the core of our being. We were walking in darkness without access to God's wisdom, but through the new birth we have transitioned into a state of full access to it. We were sinners living in righteousness, but through the new birth we have transitioned into a state of being God's righteousness, enabling us to boldly enter into His presence.

Your spirit is as holy and pure as it will be when you enter heaven.

It will not change, grow, or develop further when you get to heaven because it is perfect right now in this world. According to Ephesians 1:13, you have been sealed into Christ by the Holy Spirit; every barrier between you and the Spirit has now been removed. He is dwelling in your born-again spirit, waiting for you to acknowledge Him and allow Him to lead you into a deep, intimate relationship.

Jesus made a statement that has been translated in many different ways in John 4:24:

> God is a Spirit: and they that worship him must worship
> him in spirit and in truth.

God is a Spirit, so our relationship with Him is spirit to Spirit. He speaks to us in a still, small voice that often manifests through feeling, thoughts, or desires. The Holy Spirit speaks to our born-again spirits, and then we have to give voice to what He has said by speaking it audibly. We will discuss how to do this, and the benefits it provides us, in more detail later. Far too many struggle in their relationship with the Spirit because they do not understand what happened to them in the new birth when they made Jesus the Lord of their life.

Can I Sin?

The inquiry many people ask when they are first introduced to these truths usually involves sin. If we are holy, why do we still sin? Consider the following statement made by John in 1 John 3:9:

> Whosoever is born of God doth not commit sin; FOR
> HIS SEED REMAINETH IN HIM: AND HE CAN-
> NOT SIN, BECAUSE HE IS BORN OF GOD.

I struggled with understanding this verse for many years before realizing the three parts of my being. It is our spirit that was born again, and it is our spirit that is vacuum-packed into Jesus by the Spirit. The Holy Spirit fellowships with us through our spirit, based on our identity in Christ. His view of us is not affected by our performance or what we do for Him.

John could say a Christian "cannot sin" because he understood the realities of the new birth. We will all sin still, but that sin cannot touch our spirits, cannot penetrate the seal of the Holy Spirit. Sin for the Christian is in the flesh, or soulish realm, which is the reason John said we cannot sin. We are a spirit, and we live in a body and have a soul. Your spirit is righteous and holy, so our sins cannot change this. I know this may be difficult for you to receive at this point, but it is truth. The Holy Spirit will help you understand it just as He did for me.

The Need for Christ

Over the years, I have met many Christians who live with a sense of guilt over the things they have done in the past. They fight just as I did with accepting that a holy God could love and accept them just as they are. You may also have had similar thoughts. I struggled with this truth until I received the revelation of my spirit, soul, and body.

God can love me because He has paid the price for my sin in Christ's redemptive work. He does not love me because of my actions or the things I have done for Him. His love for me is based solely on what Christ did through His death, burial, and resurrection that opened the door for me to become a new creation and receive the Holy Spirit into my spirit.

The spirit is the new you. It has been born again, opening the door for our righteous God to accept you. When you made Jesus the

Lord of your life, the Spirit baptized you into Christ (1 Corinthians 12:13) and then sealed you with Himself (Ephesians 1:13). God now sees us through our position in Christ and, therefore, can only see us as righteous and holy because we are standing in Jesus' righteousness and holiness, not our own.

The Law was given to prove we could never be good enough for God to accept us on our own merits. It was not enough to think good thoughts, attend synagogue, or offer sacrifices at the temple. This was why Jesus had to go to the cross. My book *The Simple Message of the Cross* goes into the message of the cross and the reasons the Lord had to suffer in much more detail.

Chapter 12

Inside Out Living

For God so loved the world, that he gave his only begotten Son, that whosoever believeth in him should not perish, but have everlasting life.

JOHN 3:16

G od loves you so much that He sent Jesus to the cross. He did this to satisfy the judgment that was due for our sins and to open the door for Him to legally impart His very life into our spirits. For illustration, imagine yourself sitting in a courtroom, where your Father is the judge. The prosecution presents their case, and your Father sentences you to death and eternal separation from Him.

Can you imagine sitting in that courtroom, hearing your own Father sentence you like this? Now, imagine yourself sitting in that courtroom filled with a sense of hopelessness, knowing your sins have led you down a road from which there is no turning back. The sentence means your life is over, and you are facing an eternity separated from your Father. Can you imagine how you would feel if placed in this situation?

Now, think about your reaction if your Father stood and removed His robe after sentencing you to the harshest punishment possible. What would you think if He did this and then walked up to the bailiff and arranged to have your older brother Jesus serve your sentence in your place? The bailiff then would handcuff Jesus and escort Him out of the courtroom to serve the punishment you had been sentenced to serve.

The Born-Again Spirit Is Not Affected by Fluctuations in the Soul or Flesh

The door was opened for your spirit to be reborn by the redemptive work of Christ. It was the presentation of His blood on the heavenly mercy seat that enabled God to recreate us with a new spirit just as righteous and holy as Jesus is. The Holy Spirit vacuum-packed us or glued us together into Christ. As Paul tells us in Galatians 2:20, our life on this earth is to be lived by faith in the Son of God:

> I am crucified with Christ: nevertheless I live; yet not I,
> but Christ liveth in me: and the life which I now live in
> the flesh I live by the faith of the Son of God, who loved
> me, and gave himself for me.

Our spirits will never fluctuate, even though we may sometimes fail in our actions, thoughts, or emotions. The work done in the new birth is complete. We may get tired, cranky, or frustrated in our physical and emotional realms, but our spirits will remain righteous and holy. This is the reason the Holy Spirit dwells in our spirits, and it is also why we are now able to access Him any time we want.

We have already looked at 1 John 4:17, which tells us we are identical to Jesus in this world and is speaking of our born-again spirit. The Gospels reveal a very close working relationship between Jesus and the Holy Spirit, which we will examine in later chapters. If our born-again spirit is identical to Jesus, wouldn't this mean we can have the same working relationship with the Spirit today as the Lord did?

The Revelation of the New Birth

The revelation of the new birth provides a foundation for us to enter into a relationship with the Holy Spirit. He wants to spend time with us but is often limited by our lack of understanding that we have been made righteous and are no longer sinners or even have a sinful nature. If you can get ahold of the things we have discussed in these first chapters, you will find your relationship with the Spirit to follow almost naturally.

In hindsight, it was my lack of understanding that I was righteous and holy as a result of my spirit becoming a new creation which caused me to be hesitant in my approach to God. My prayer life suffered because I did not have a clear understanding that I had been made worthy to stand in God's presence and fellowship with the Spirit. The Holy Spirit helped me through my battles and opened my eyes to the truth of my identity in Christ, and He will do the same for you.

Satan will try his best to convince you of your unworthiness to approach God, reminding you of your sins and mistakes but will never speak of your true identity in Christ. If you will commit time to meditating on the truths mentioned in these opening chapters, he will be unsuccessful in his efforts to do so. Your spiritual experience will no longer be like riding on a roller coaster, and you will find your relationship with the Spirit of God growing almost effortlessly.

The Fruit of Our Born-Again Spirit

My early experiences as a Christian seemed at times as if I was riding a roller coaster. I would experience an emotional high in service and feel as if I could overcome anything. However, this would last at the most one or two days, and then situations and life events would cause me to crest and seemingly hit rock bottom. The Holy Spirit would help me as much as He could but was limited by the fact that I was viewing myself through the lens of my flesh and not through my spiritual identity, based on who I was in Christ.

I believe the revelation of your identity in Christ will bring freedom to you just as it has me, and it was in this revelation the Holy Spirit first revealed Himself to me. He will do the same for you. You were joined to the Lord in the new birth and have become one spirit with Him (1 Corinthians 6:17). As you learn more and more about the Spirit, you will find yourself becoming dependent on Him, which will, in turn, lead you into the place God ordained for you to walk.

Paul provides us with a list we often refer to as the fruit of the Spirit in Galatians 5:22-23: love, joy, peace, longsuffering, goodness, faith, meekness, and temperance. These are all the fruit of your born-again spirit, reflecting the Spirit who lives within you. It does not matter how you feel, how negative your circumstances seem to be, or how negative people may treat you, these fruits are in your spirit. They are the fruit of your born-again spirit and will never fluctuate or decrease.

Some of you may be asking how it is possible to have joy in your spirit while feeling miserable. The answer lies in the three parts of our being. Joy is a fruit of our born-again spirit, while misery is the fruit of an unrenewed soul. We have been sealed in Christ with the Holy Spirit, and our born-again spirit will never fluctuate. It is righteous and holy. Our spirits are full of the fruit of the spirit, and the choice to renew our minds with the Word of God is ours alone to make. The Holy Spirit will help us but never force us to spend time meditating on Scripture.

Living from the Spirit

But ye are not in the flesh, but in the Spirit, if so be
that the Spirit of God dwell in you. Now if any man
have not the Spirit of Christ, he is none of his.

ROMANS 8:9

Every Christian has been sealed with the Holy Spirit, and their position in Christ will never change. Our sins, our mistakes, or anything that comes against us cannot change this. If you have made Jesus the Lord of your life, your spirit has been recreated and will never change. Your relationship with the Holy Spirit is based on this truth, and you will continue to struggle in this area until you come to an understanding of these foundational truths we have been discussing.

The flesh realm does exist; I am not denying this as some ministers teach. We do live in a natural body, but we do not have to let it rule us. The person with a revelation of who they are in Christ as a result of the new birth will walk in authority over their soul and body. I believe this is what Paul is telling us in Romans 8. The Holy Spirit can live in our spirit only because it has been recreated and is as righteous and holy as Jesus is in this world.

Chapter 13

An Eternal Redemption

*But Christ being come an high priest of good things to come, by a
greater and more perfect tabernacle, not made with hands, that
is to say, not of this building; neither by the blood of goats and
calves, but by his own blood he entered in once into the holy
place, having obtained eternal redemption for us. For if the blood
of bulls and of goats, and the ashes of an heifer sprinkling the
unclean, sanctifieth to the purifying of the flesh: how much more
shall the blood of Christ, who through the eternal Spirit offered
himself without spot to God, purge your conscience from dead works
to serve the living God? And for this cause he is the mediator of
the new testament, that by means of death, for the redemption of
the transgressions that were under the first testament, they which
are called might receive the promise of eternal inheritance.*

HEBREWS 9:11-15

Our relationship with the Holy Spirit is built out of our spiritual identity. Far too many Christians I've met over the years live through their emotional and physical identities and struggle with understanding the Spirit and His ministry as a result. You must never forget God is a spirit (John 4:24) and views you through your identity in Christ in the spirit realm. The challenge I've faced, more often than not, in teaching about the Holy Spirit is very few people in our churches understand this foundational truth.

We have already read Ephesians 4:24 and 1 John 4:17 and seen our spirits were created in true righteousness and holiness; they are identical to Jesus in this world as a result. From a spiritual perspective, we are not becoming more and more like Him. The moment we confessed Jesus as Lord, our spirits were born again and became new creations (2 Corinthians 5:17) who are identical spiritually to the Lord in this world.

Our Identity Is in Christ

We are identical to Christ in this world because our spirits were sealed into Him with the Holy Spirit (Ephesians 1:13) the moment we made Him our Lord. Our standing before God is based on Christ's redemptive work, and it is because we are now in Christ that God sees Jesus when He looks at us. Being sealed with the Holy Spirit into Christ ensures our standing before the throne of God and also provides us access to His faith, His nature, His ability, and His Spirit.

I have heard people ask why they can't just live like the devil if they are sealed in Christ and sin no longer can affect the status of our spirits. After all, sin cannot penetrate our spirits so why do those of us in the ministry put so much emphasis on doing what is right and living holy lives? These are all good questions that need to be answered if our goal is to develop a relationship with the Holy Spirit.

A New Covenant

The book of Hebrews offers much insight into the answer to questions about why we should live holy lives, presenting much insight into the New Covenant in which you and I live. The Old Covenant focused on human performance, but the new is focused on Jesus' performance in His death, burial, and resurrection. We will never develop any level of intimacy with the Spirit without first getting out of the Old Covenant way of thinking.

The New Covenant deals with humanity based on faith and the transformation that occurred in our spirits. Our relationship with God and His Spirit is based solely on this. Hebrews 9:11-15 provides us a picture of Christ presenting His blood in heavenly tabernacle and obtaining an eternal redemption through it. Unfortunately, we are not teaching these truths correctly, and most Christians are unaware of this fact and think our relationship with God is based on our performance.

You need to understand your relationship with the Holy Spirit is based on Christ's redemptive work alone, which is eternal, steadfast, and sure. It is because of this fact you can now approach God boldly without any fear of rejection (Hebrews 4:16) and experience a level of intimacy with Him that simply was not possible while living under the Old Covenant. Notice the question asked by the author of Hebrews in Hebrews 10:1-2:

> For the law having a shadow of good things to come, and not the very image of the things, can never with those sacrifices which they offered year by year continually make the comers thereunto perfect. FOR THEN WOULD THEY NOT HAVE CEASED TO BE OFFERED? because that the worshippers once purged should have had no more conscience of sins.

Old Testament sacrifices were needed to cover sin, but they could only provide temporary covering. A new offering was needed for every new sin, which led to a persistent consciousness of sin. Each one was a reminder of the need for a permanent sacrifice that would offer a means of escape from the sin nature plaguing humanity.

A Contrast Between the Old and New Covenants

The book of Hebrews provides a contrast between the Old and New Covenants. The Old required sacrifices for sin to be made continually, so every time a person sinned, they had to offer a sacrifice to atone for their sin. Once a year, on the Day of Atonement, a sacrifice was made for the nation. The Old Covenant was essentially designed by God to continuously remind people of their need for a Savior.

While there was a need for a continuous shedding of blood in the Old Covenant, the New only needed a single sacrifice: Jesus died once for all. His death was the one sacrifice that paid the penalty for the sin of every human being for all time. The Old Covenant sacrifices could not completely atone for sin, but the sinless blood of Jesus could. His blood dealt with the issue of sin, ending all barriers between us and God for all time. I believe this is what the writer of Hebrews is speaking of in Hebrews 10:8-14:

> Above when he said, Sacrifice and offering and burnt offerings and offering for sin thou wouldest not, neither hadst pleasure therein; which are offered by the law; then said he, Lo, I come to do thy will, O God. He taketh away the first, that he may establish the second. By the which will we are sanctified through the offering of the body of Jesus Christ once for all. And every priest standeth daily ministering and offering oftentimes the same sacrifices, which can never take away sins: but this man, after he had offered one sacrifice for sins for ever, sat down on the

right hand of God; from henceforth expecting till his ene-
mies be made his footstool. For by one offering he hath
perfected for ever them that are sanctified.

Jesus offered one sacrifice with His life and blood for all sin for
all time; it was through this He obtained eternal redemption. When
you accepted Him as your Lord, He did not just deal with sins you
had committed until that moment. His sacrifice dealt with every sin
you will ever commit and offered forgiveness for each one before you
had a chance to commit them!

We see in Hebrews 10:14 it was "by one offering He has perfected forever those who are being sanctified" (NKJV). This is telling
us through the offering of Jesus we have been perfected forever, not
just until we commit our next sin. You will not be able to benefit
from this or experience anything provided in His redemptive work
living according to the input of the physical or emotional parts of
your being.

Jesus told His disciples in John 14:26 the Holy Spirit would be sent
to teach them "all things." You will never fully gain revelation of your
spiritual identity and all that has been provided through Christ's sacrifice without His help. I've found people struggle with understanding Him and receiving His help until they understand the change
that occurred in their spirits when they made Jesus the Lord of their
lives, resulting in them being born again.

Chapter 14

Our Eternal Standing with God

God is a Spirit: and they that worship him must
worship him in spirit and in truth.

JOHN 4:24

I have yet to meet a Christian who disagrees that God can do anything; this fact is beyond question. While we all agree on His ability, many of us struggle with doubt regarding His willingness to act on our behalf because we feel we don't deserve anything from Him. It's true that none of us truly "deserve" anything from God, which is why understanding the three parts of our being is so important. The part of our being that changed was not our physical body or our soul—which consists of our personality, mind, will, and emotions—but our spirit. Our spirits have been recreated and are now righteous, holy, and pure.

From the Spirit

Jesus told the woman at the well in Samaria that true worshipers would worship in "spirit and in truth" (John 4:24). God is a spirit, and true worship flows from our born-again spirits. We will never overcome our feelings of unworthiness to serve God or to receive from Him without first learning to relate to Him based on our new spiritual identity, which is solely rooted in Christ's redemptive work.

I personally struggled with my sense of worthiness to receive anything from God. However, it was the revelation of who I had become in Christ Jesus that transformed my understanding. The Holy Spirit guided me through Scripture, revealing the work He accomplished in my spirit when I was born again. He helped me realize that my spirit is now joined to the Lord and in union with God. God accepts us based on this union and our position in Christ.

In Ephesians 4:24, we see that God created our new spirits in righteousness and true holiness. The Holy Spirit baptized us into Jesus and sealed us, ensuring that we are secure in Him. God has enveloped us in Jesus with His Spirit because He knew we would never be able to maintain our salvation on our own. Some people mistakenly believe that being born again is merely God picking them up, forgiving their past sins, dusting them off, and pointing them in the right direction. In reality, it is so much more than that.

Perfected Forever

Salvation is much more than just a new beginning. If all God did was forgive our sins and give us a fresh start, we would likely ruin it, just as Adam did when he sinned in the Garden of Eden (Genesis 3:1-7). Every human being has "sinned, and come short of the glory of God" (Romans 3:23). As a Christian, while my spirit has been recreated, my soul and body still need attention.

Some people approach their relationship with God as if He grades on a curve. They emphasize the good works they have done as if those actions can earn them His favor. However, every person who has been born again is granted right standing with God. This is part of being righteous, holy, and pure. Our spirits have been recreated, immersed in Christ, and sealed in Him. God now views us through Christ's redemptive work, rather than through our good or bad deeds.

Hebrews 10:14 tells us that we were sanctified forever by Christ's one offering of Himself. Through His death, burial, and resurrection, we have been perfected for all time. Some teach that Christians lose our salvation every time we sin, but this is incorrect. God saves us only once. You are sealed in Jesus and cannot lose your standing with your heavenly Father as a result.

Forgiven for All Time

I believe it is important to confess our sins. According to 1 John 1:9, God is faithful and just to forgive us and cleanse us from all unrighteousness when we do so. There are no alternative routes with Him. The blood of Jesus was shed once, providing eternal redemption for every person who will ever live (Hebrews 9:12-28). Christians confess their sins not to regain their salvation but to close any openings for Satan to work in their lives.

Romans 6:16 provides further insight:

> Know ye not, that to whom ye yield yourselves servants
> to obey, his servants ye are to whom ye obey; whether of
> sin unto death, or of obedience unto righteousness?

Repentance involves purposely turning away from the devil and his lies. It is an admission to God that we were wrong for yielding to the devil and acting on the thoughts he placed in our minds. When we do this, we return to the right standing we already have with Him in our spirits, and we break Satan's dominion over our lives.

Do not let Satan condemn you for your mistakes. We have all made

foolish choices that embarrass us. One of the issues I have observed
is that Christians often allow the enemy to convince them they have
committed a new offense. You will never commit a sin that surprises
God. He saw your sins before you were born and sent Jesus to the
cross two thousand years ago to pay the price for every one of them.
That is where your forgiveness was given for all time.

The only way God could not forgive a sin you have committed is
if Jesus had not gone to the cross. If Jesus had to return to the cross
for every sin, He never would have come down from it, been buried, or risen again. His one death, one burial, and one resurrection
provided forgiveness of sin for all time. This is the foundation of our
identity in Christ, and it is the Holy Spirit who was sent to reveal
this foundational truth to us.

Can We Lose Our Salvation?

I was raised in a denomination that believed it was impossible to
"lose" our salvation. Since they did not have altar calls, my parents
assumed that my brother, sister, and I were all saved. However, I can
say that I most definitely was not. The church where I finally surrendered to the Lord was completely different from the one I grew
up in. In that new church, they believed that salvation could be lost
every time we sinned, leading to a constant need to go to the altar
to "rededicate" ourselves to God.

I want to address the question of whether our salvation is eternally
secure or can be lost, using Hebrews 6:4-6 as a reference:

> For it is impossible for those who were once enlightened,
> and have tasted of the heavenly gift, and were made par-
> takers of the Holy Ghost, and have tasted the good word
> of God, and the powers of the world to come, if they shall

fall away, to renew them again unto repentance; seeing they crucify to themselves the Son of God afresh, and put him to an open shame.

Verse 4 states that "it is impossible" for those who have been saved and then fall away to return to the Lord. I spent many years meditating on this verse, seeking guidance from the Holy Spirit to understand its meaning. My focus was on two opposing views of salvation that I had been taught: one that claims salvation is eternally secure and another that suggests salvation can be lost with each sin. One day, the Spirit answered me in a surprising way, saying, "Neither view is correct."

Five Qualifications

From this revelation, I learned the importance of allowing the Holy Spirit to offer a perspective that goes beyond my previous considerations. He revealed to me five qualifications that must be met before a person reaches a point where they cannot be restored to a relationship with God.

1. "For it is impossible for those who were once enlightened." This refers to the revelation of our need for salvation. John 6:44 states that no one can come to Jesus unless they are first drawn by the Holy Spirit. He must illuminate the understanding for a person to perceive their need for salvation.

2. "And have tasted of the heavenly gift." I believe this is a reference to salvation. The Holy Spirit drew us to Jesus, enlightened our spiritual understanding, and then baptized us into Jesus when we responded.

3. "And were made partakers of the Holy Ghost." I believe this is speaking of the baptism with the Spirit, an experience we will discuss in the next section.

4. "And have tasted the good word of God." This is speaking of the person who has moved beyond salvation, been baptized with the Holy Spirit, and gotten into the Word of God. They are moving deeper into their relationship with the Spirit and beginning to receive revelation knowledge from Him.

5. "And the powers of the world to come." This is a place of full maturity in which we begin to see the Holy Spirit's gifts begin to flow in our lives.

Christians might reach a point where they could renounce their salvation. This decision is not made lightly or in an instant. The Holy Spirit continues to work in the lives of individuals who choose to turn away from the Lord and toward the world. It can take years for our hearts to become so hardened against God that returning to Him becomes impossible. This process does not happen overnight, despite what some Christians may believe.

Chapter 15

The Cost of Sin Imputed to Jesus

Blessed is he whose transgression is forgiven, whose sin is covered. Blessed is the man unto whom the LORD imputeth not iniquity, and in whose spirit there is no guile.

PSALM 32:1-2

The word "impute" is an accounting term. When you provide a credit card to purchase goods at a store, the charge is "imputed" to your credit card company's account. The actual bill for those goods isn't paid until you make a payment to the card issuer. Similarly, those who have accepted Jesus as the Lord of their lives have had the "cost" of their sins "imputed" to Jesus' account. He paid that debt with His blood.

Eternally Secure?

The cost of your sin was imputed to Jesus' account and paid with His blood. You received a righteous, holy spirit that has been sanctified and perfected forever when you were born again. It was the payment made by Jesus that made this possible. Every Christian has received a spirit that is righteous, holy, and sealed into Christ. We were placed

into the Lord (1 Corinthians 12:13) when we accepted Jesus as our
Lord and then sealed into Jesus by the Holy Spirit (Ephesians 1:13),
providing us a new identity.

No Christian has ever been forced into salvation. God extends
the offer to save us from sin, but His offer must be accepted before
any person will be born again. He also will not make us stay saved.
In John 10:29, Jesus said "no man is able to pluck" those who have
received Him from "my Father's hand." Sometimes people will use
this statement to say it is impossible for a person who has been saved
to lose their salvation.

I agree it is impossible to lose our salvation. No one can pluck us
out of the hand of God. Nobody can take us from Him, but in Scripture, you can never find a situation where He forces people to do
things against their will. As we discussed at the end of the last chapter, you cannot be plucked out of God's hand, but you can choose
to get out of it yourself.

The Path to a Reprobate Mind

In the previous chapter, we examined Hebrews 6:4-6, which states
that it is impossible for a person who has fallen away from their salvation to return to God. This passage suggests that someone who
turns away from their faith cannot be saved again, contradicting the
idea that one can lose their salvation and be saved multiple times,
as some teachings suggest. Once salvation is lost, returning to God
becomes impossible.

I outlined five qualifications in the last chapter that must be met
before anyone loses their place in Christ and reaches a point where
returning to Him is no longer an option. Our understanding of
spiritual maturity often differs significantly from what is depicted
in Hebrews 6:4-6. A person who ultimately loses their salvation will

have spent years making choices that resist the Holy Spirit, which gradually hardens their hearts against Him.

In Romans 1, Paul addresses individuals who have hardened their hearts toward God and the consequences of their actions. In verse 24, he explains, "God also gave them up to uncleanness through the lusts of their own hearts." This shows that God did not force them to pursue their own desires; rather, they chose to turn away from Him, and He respected their decisions.

The Reprobate Mind

And even as they did not like to retain God in their knowledge, God gave them over to a reprobate mind, to do those things which are not convenient.

ROMANS 1:28

In this verse, Paul explains that a reprobate mind develops when people do not "like to retain God in their knowledge." To retain God in our understanding, we must spend time each day with the Holy Spirit and engage with the Word of God. John 6:44 reminds us that it is impossible to come to the Father unless we are drawn to Him, and it is the Holy Spirit who plays this crucial role. The more time we dedicate to nurturing our relationship with God and Jesus through the Holy Spirit, the deeper that relationship will become.

A reprobate mind reflects a soul that has become hardened against God, making it incapable of discerning right from wrong. However, those who develop a relationship with the Holy Spirit will not walk the path that leads to a reprobate mind. Their connection with both the Holy Spirit and the Word of God will help ensure they stay on the path that God has called them to walk.

Do You Have a Reprobate Mind?

A person who disciplines themselves to cultivate a relationship with the Spirit and the Word will quickly repent and turn to God when they sin. In contrast, someone who does not acknowledge the Spirit's presence and only makes a partial or lesser commitment to the Word will not be as swift to repent after sinning. I believe this description aligns with the individual Paul refers to in Romans 1:28 who fails to retain the knowledge of God in their soul.

Those who choose not to hold onto the knowledge of God may eventually reach a point where God allows them to go their own way, leading to the development of a reprobate mind. I have spoken with individuals who feared they had reached this stage. It is important to understand that someone who has truly crossed this line will not feel any conviction about the things of God. The mere concern about developing a reprobate mind serves as evidence that one has not yet reached that point.

It is scriptural to say that you have been saved, sanctified, and perfected forever. However, you cannot indulge in sin. A person who does so opens the door for Satan to work in their life and allows their heart to become hardened against the prompting of the Holy Spirit. This process will include losing sight of our spiritual identity, which is based on being sealed in Christ (Ephesians 1:13).

Spirit, Soul, and Body

I believe that understanding our spirit, soul, and body is essential for grasping our spiritual identity. When you were born again, you were "made the righteousness of God in [Christ]" (2 Corinthians 5:21). Your born-again spirit was created "in righteous and true holiness" (Ephesians 4:24) and is identical to Jesus (1 John 4:17). This foundational revelation can unlock your relationship with the Father, Son, and Holy Spirit.

Your identity in Christ is based on being sealed in Him by the Spirit, not on your actions. Sin cannot affect your born-again spirit. Some people accuse those of us who teach these truths of giving a license to sin. It's crucial to understand that every sin has been forgiven and cannot change your standing before God. However, this doesn't mean we should tolerate sin in our lives. Unaddressed sin can create barriers in our souls, hindering our relationship with the Holy Spirit.

Romans 6:16 tells us that we become servants to whomever we yield ourselves. When someone allows sin into their life, they yield to Satan. This is not a position any Christian should desire. Satan is the author of all sin, and we avoid sin not to prevent God from rejecting us; He has sanctified and perfected us forever. Instead, we avoid sin to remain fully yielded and sensitive to the Holy Spirit's work in our lives.

A Yoke of Bondage

God is spirit. He sees us in the spiritual realm and is pleased with us because we are His creation. His love for us is not based on our actions. This love was demonstrated more than two thousand years ago when Jesus went to the cross to pay for all sins. Our salvation is secure, and no one can take us out of His hand. While Satan cannot cause us to lose our salvation, he can gain access to introduce sickness, disease, poverty, and depression into our lives if we open the door by yielding to sin.

Paul made a relevant statement in Galatians 5:1:

> Stand fast therefore in the liberty wherewith Christ hath made us free, and be not entangled again with the yoke of bondage.

The yoke of bondage he refers to is a performance based mentality. Do not allow Satan to deceive you into thinking God loves you only when you perform well. I fell into this trap in my early years as have many Christians. It will lead you into a mindset based on Old Testament Law believing God can only love us if we do right. We must never forget His acceptance is based solely on Christ's death, burial, and resurrection. It will never be based on our performance.

Resist the Devil

Christ has set us free (Galatians 5:1) from the Law; however, this freedom does not give us permission to live in sin. As discussed in this chapter, sin opens the door for Satan to operate in our lives. It prevents us from fully experiencing the benefits of our spiritual identity, which is rooted in our position of being sealed in Christ.

Peter warns us that Satan is going about as "a roaring lion, seeking whom he may devour" (1 Peter 5:8, NKJV). When someone submits to his schemes, they open themselves up to being devoured by Satan through sickness, disease, lack, and oppression. Although the Holy Spirit will never leave us, His ability to assist us can be hindered if we choose to ignore Him and instead pursue worldly things that create a barrier between us and the Holy Spirit.

Sin is deadly. The wrath of God has been satisfied by Jesus in His redemptive work, but the wrath of Satan has not. Satan will take advantage of you in any way you allow him to. He has no authority over you beyond that which you yield to him. The primary way we yield is through ignorance. This is the reason it is vital we dedicate time each day to meditate on the Word and spend time fellowshipping with the Holy Spirit discussing the things we have been meditating on.

BAPTIZED WITH THE SPIRIT AND FIRE

I indeed baptize you with water unto repentance.
But he that cometh after me is mightier than
I, whose shoes I am not worthy to bear: he shall
baptize you with the Holy Ghost, and with fire.

MATTHEW 3:11

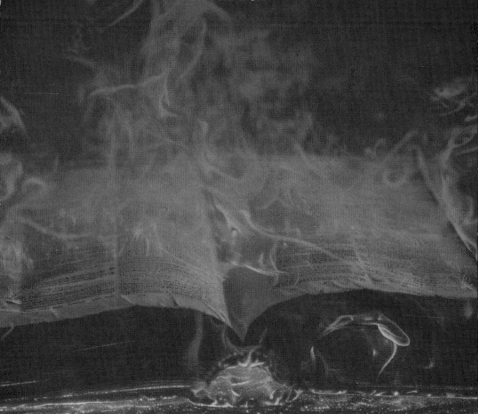

Chapter 16

The Promise of the Father

And, being assembled together with them, commanded them
that they should not depart from Jerusalem, but wait for
the promise of the Father, which, saith he, ye have heard
of me. For John truly baptized with water; but ye shall be
baptized with the Holy Ghost not many days hence.

ACTS 1:4-5

We have already seen in John 20:22 Jesus breathed the Holy Spirit into the disciples' spirits in His first appearance to them after the resurrection. This was the moment they were filled with the Spirit and became new creations in Christ. The Spirit had entered into their spirits at that moment, just as He has entered every person since who has believed in their heart and confessed Jesus as their Lord and Savior (Romans 10:9-10).

Jesus appeared to His disciples for another forty days (Acts 1:3) before ascending to the Father (Acts 1:9-11). Prior to the ascension, He commanded them to "wait for the promise of the Father," speaking of the baptism with the Holy Spirit. As I mentioned at the end of chapter 1, this clearly shows there is a second experience beyond salvation as Jesus' command to wait was directed to people already born again and filled with the Spirit.

Waiting for the Father's Promise

On the surface, it did not make sense for Jesus to tell His disciples to wait to be baptized with the Holy Spirit before moving forth into ministry. They had traveled with Him for just over three years and spent forty days with Him after the resurrection. News had gotten out about Jesus being raised from the dead, and it was what people were talking about. The world was literally buzzing with this news, and it seemed like a perfect time for the disciples to launch their ministries.

People had seen Jesus. The disciples had eaten with Him, and He invited Thomas to stick his finger into the holes in His hands from the nails of the crucifixion. The disciples literally had physical proof in Jesus' resurrection, and they had the greatest message to be told. With all of this going for the disciples, can you imagine their shock when Jesus announced His soon departure and commanded them to wait in Jerusalem before stepping into ministry?

The Greatest Message and the Power

The disciples had received the Holy Spirit when Jesus breathed Him into their spirits and had had been trained by the Lord personally for ministry. If anyone had been ready to launch into ministry, I would think it would have been the disciples. They were far more qualified for ministry according to the standards typically set today for ministers in our churches; however, this was not enough though for them to qualify. Jesus told them to wait until they received power after being baptized with the Holy Spirit.

Jesus had been resurrected from the dead, so His disciples had the greatest message to deliver. He had given them the Gospel message, and it was fresh and real. The people they would preach to had been physically present and saw the crucifixion with their own eyes or heard of it from someone who was there. If this were not enough, the book of Matthew tells us that many saints were resurrected at the same time as Jesus and had already prepared the ground for the disciples' ministries in Matthew 27:51-56:

> And, behold, the veil of the temple was rent in twain from the top to the bottom; and the earth did quake, and the rocks rent; and the graves were opened; and many bodies of the saints which slept arose, and came out of the graves after his resurrection, and went into the holy city, and appeared unto many. Now when the centurion, and they that were with him, watching Jesus, saw the earthquake, and those things that were done, they feared greatly, saying, Truly this was the Son of God. And many women were there beholding afar off, which followed Jesus from Galilee, ministering unto him: among which was Mary Magdalene, and Mary the mother of James and Joses, and the mother of Zebedees children.

A mass resurrection literally occurred when Jesus was raised from the dead! Can you imagine how many people were talking about their dead relatives they had buried suddenly showing up alive? That alone had to be something the people were talking about. It would have been a prime opportunity to preach the Gospel from our perspective, but Jesus told His disciples to wait for the Holy Spirit to emerge.

Our Power or His?

I believe Jesus' last command to His disciples leaves a message for us that most seem to miss today. We lead people through a simple salvation prayer, hand them a stack of tracts, and send them off to win the world without the Holy Spirit or His power. In a very real sense, isn't this a violation of the command given to the disciples in Acts 1?

No Christian should be witnessing for the Lord in their own effort or ability, but most do; this is a very unfortunate truth that very few are willing to talk about or even acknowledge. Every member of the body of Christ should wait until they are baptized with the Holy Spirit and endued with His power before sharing the Gospel message with others. This was the Lord's last command, and I believe we need to take it much more seriously.

There is an interesting set of verses in John 2:23-25 that I believe applies to our discussion:

> Now when he was in Jerusalem at the passover, in the feast day, many believed in his name, when they saw the miracles which he did. But Jesus did not commit himself unto them, because he knew all men, and needed not that any should testify of man: for he knew what was in man.

Do you agree that Jesus came to this earth to turn as many people as possible to the Father? If this was true, why wouldn't He accept all of those people who flocked to His meetings? The people saw the miracle, multitudes believed Him, and others were ready to testify, but He was unwilling to make any level of commitment to them.

Jesus did not want anyone testifying about Him in their own ability. His command to the disciples to wait for the Spirit was issued at the end of His ministry, while the incident in John 2 occurred at the beginning. Jesus was consistent in His insistence, from the beginning of His ministry to the earthly end of it, that no one should serve Him or share what we call the Gospel message today without first being endued with power by the Holy Spirit.

A Supernatural Ministry

God intended for the Gospel message to be preached with the supernatural anointing of His Spirit, intending for it to be accompanied by signs and wonders. We see this in Jesus' final statement before the ascension, which is recorded in Mark 16:14-20:

> Afterward he appeared unto the eleven as they sat at meat, and upbraided them with their unbelief and hardness of heart, because they believed not them which had seen him after he was risen. And he said unto them, Go ye into all the world, and preach the gospel to every creature. He that believeth and is baptized shall be saved; but he that believeth not shall be damned. AND THESE SIGNS SHALL FOLLOW THEM THAT BELIEVE; In my name shall they cast out devils; they shall speak with new tongues; they shall take up serpents; and if they drink any deadly thing, it shall not hurt them; they shall lay hands on the sick, and they shall recover. So then after the Lord had spoken unto them, he was received up into heaven, and sat on the right hand of God. And they went forth, and preached every where, the Lord working with them, and confirming the word with signs following. Amen.

There is a large segment of the body of Christ today who do not believe signs and wonders are for us today; we will deal with this in a later chapter. For now, let me ask you a question. If Jesus promised those early disciples to confirm the Word they preached with signs, why wouldn't we need Him to confirm the Word we preached in the same way?

God Confirmed Jesus' Message
with Signs and Wonders

Did you know that even Jesus needed signs and wonders to confirm
His ministry? We see this in Hebrews 2:1-4:

> Therefore we ought to give the more earnest heed to the
> things which we have heard, lest at any time we should
> let them slip. For if the word spoken by angels was sted-
> fast, and every transgression and disobedience received
> a just recompence of reward; how shall we escape, if we
> neglect so great salvation; which at the first began to be
> spoken by the Lord, and was confirmed unto us by them
> that heard him; GOD ALSO BEARING THEM WIT-
> NESS, BOTH WITH SIGNS AND WONDERS, AND
> WITH DIVERS MIRACLES, AND GIFTS OF THE
> HOLY GHOST, according to his own will?

These verses tell us God confirmed the message Jesus preached
"with signs and wonders, with various miracles, and gifts of the Holy
Spirit" (NKJV). We saw in Mark 16:20 the Lord worked with the disciples and confirmed their message with signs and wonders. Do you
think it is slightly arrogant to say we have grown beyond the point
to where we no longer need God to do the same for us today?

Chapter 17

The Foundation of Revelation Knowledge

But the Comforter, which is the Holy Ghost, whom
the Father will send in my name, he shall teach
you all things, and bring all things to your
remembrance, whatsoever I have said unto you.

JOHN 14:26

The baptism with the Spirit is the cornerstone on which every aspect of our relationship with the Holy Spirit is built. This was a statement I would have argued against early in my Christian journey. As I've grown in my relationship with the Spirit over the years, my perspective has changed, becoming clear how important the baptism is for those who want to become tuned to the Holy Spirit and enter into intimate fellowship with Him.

You will often hear people talk about the baptism with the Spirit with the evidence of speaking in tongues. I believe it is true that one proof of evidence of the baptism is a supernatural prayer language, which we will talk about in this section. For myself, the most valuable result of being baptized with the Spirit was in how it opened the door for me to receive revelation directly from the Holy Spirit.

Our Divine Teacher

Revelation knowledge is different from knowledge gained through self-effort. We are all capable of studying any subject and memorizing facts, and some of us have more natural abilities in certain areas than others. The knowledge received from the Spirit though is not something any of us can receive by putting our noses to the proverbial grindstone and studying. It does not matter the number of hours you put into studying Scripture or the number of verses you memorize. Revelation knowledge cannot be gained through self-effort.

I am not saying we do not need to study Scripture or memorize verses. The Bible is not a natural book; it holds the perfect representation of God's Word. As you study its contents, there will be moments when it will come alive as the Spirit quickens the information to you. When this happens, a verse you may have struggled to understand for years will suddenly become clear. I have found myself wondering why I struggle at times with a verse when this happens. While this does happen for those who have not been baptized with the Spirit, it happens far less often than for those who have received the baptism.

We see in John 14:26 the Spirit was sent to teach us all things, specifically, the Word of God, and this verse has become a mainstay in my life and ministry. The Holy Spirit was sent to teach us and reveal Scripture to us to prepare us for ministry. I believe the main difference between a person who acknowledges His presence and presses into relationship with Him and a person who does not is the revelation of God's Word received from Him. The reason for this is because those who do not acknowledge the Spirit haven't opened themselves up to their Divine Teacher.

My Experience with the
Spirit in Bible College

I once had a professor in college who had multiple degrees in theological studies, having spent more than thirty years studying Scripture. It would absolutely infuriate him when I would explain a passage of Scripture in class that he had studied for years and read multiple commentaries about without coming to a clear understanding. My explanations came from revelation received during times of fellowship with the Spirit of God. My professor ended up failing me in the class because the students in class started asking me questions instead of him.

There was nothing magical about the things I shared with my fellow students. I just went to the Holy Spirit and asked Him to help me understand the things we were studying in class, and He did. The college as an institution did not believe the baptism with the Spirit to be a valid experience for our day, but several of my classmates received the baptism as a result of what they saw in my life. It was not that I had anything in my own abilities or knowledge to offer that drew their attention.

In the mind of my professor, I was an ignoramus, and he did not view me as being intelligent, so he wanted to reject the things I shared in class. The struggle with doing this was the things I received from the Holy Spirit made sense to him and opened his understanding of verses he had spent untold hours studying without coming to a clear understanding of their meaning. He asked me one day in class what references I was using. When I responded that I was not using any commentary but spending time praying in tongues over those particular Scriptures, it absolutely irritated him.

A Burning Fire

One of the most notable changes when I was baptized with the Spirit was it created a hunger for God's Word in me that was almost unsatiable. I was going to college, working full time, and spending six to eight hours every day studying Scripture and praying in tongues: this went on for years. The Word of God literally exploded inside of me, reminding me of Jeremiah 20:9 when I think of those early years:

> Then I said, I will not make mention of him, nor speak any more in his name. But HIS WORD WAS IN MINE HEART AS A BURNING FIRE SHUT UP IN MY BONES, and I was weary with forbearing, and I could not stay.

The prophet Jeremiah had gotten tired of being persecuted and rejected by those God sent him to minister to. He decided to stop speaking what God was giving him but found that was not possible. The Word of God burned within him to where he was unable to keep it to himself. This is exactly how I feel but recognize there may be some who read this book who have never had the Word of God come alive like this to them. If this describes you, look no further than the ministry of the Spirit. He was sent to teach you, and the baptism with the Spirit is the open door through which you can enter into relationship with Him.

The Spirit and Revelation Knowledge

The baptism with the Spirit is the door through which we enter into an intimate relationship with the Spirit of God. If you have never received the experience, that is probably why the Word of God has never come alive in your life. It is the ministry of the Spirit to the truths of Scripture and to make them come alive in our hearts. Revelation knowledge is the fruit of His work in our hearts. With this in mind, notice once again what Jesus said about the Holy Spirit's ministry in John 14:26:

But the Comforter, which is the Holy Ghost, whom the Father will send in my name, HE SHALL TEACH YOU ALL THINGS, AND BRING ALL THINGS TO YOUR REMEMBRANCE, whatsoever I have said unto you.

One of the main reasons God sent the Spirit to be with us is to teach us and to impart a revelation of Jesus to our hearts. I find the more time spent praying in tongues, the clearer the redemptive work of Christ becomes to me. Paul speaks of the believer praying in tongues as speaking mysteries in 1 Corinthians 14:2. He also referred to the mystery as "Christ in you, the hope of glory" in Colossians 1:27. It is through the baptism with the Spirit we are given the ability to pray out this mystery and receive an impartation of God's wisdom.

Chapter 18

The Holy Spirit and Fire

*I indeed baptize you with water unto repentance. but he that
cometh after me is mightier than I, whose shoes I am not worthy
to bear: he shall baptize you with the Holy Ghost, and with fire*

MATTHEW 3:11

The word *baptism* means to submerge or immerse, and every
Christian needs to be submerged and immersed in the Holy
Spirit. This is the experience in which we turn everything over to
Him and begin to experience His teaching ministry in such a way that
the Word of God begins to come alive. It is also the door through
which we enter to begin walking in all of His other gifts, such as
speaking in tongues, the word of wisdom, gifts of healing, and working of miracles.

The New Birth and the Baptism

There are many advantages to being baptized with the Holy Spirit.
Jesus placed such a value on the experience that His last command
to the disciples, prior to departing, was for them to wait for it before
moving forward into ministry (Acts 1:4-5). There are a lot of groups
who openly speak against this experience; I grew up attending a

church that was one of them. Without realizing it, the church was openly encouraging members to disobey the Lord's final command.

Keep in mind I am not out to criticize any group. Most of those who oppose the baptism with the Spirit do so because they have been taught that they received all the Spirit when they were born again. They are sincere in their opposition but sincerely wrong. This does not mean they are not good people or are doing their best to live godly lives. I've actually met many wonderful people in churches that do not believe in the baptism Jesus spoke of in Acts 1.

So far, we spent the beginning of this book examining the change that occurred when we were born again. The disciples first received the Holy Spirit when Jesus breathed Himself into their spirits in the first resurrection appearance (John 20:22). Their spirits were made new (2 Corinthians 5:17) at that moment just as ours are today when we receive Jesus to be our Lord and Savior. They received the Spirit into their spirits at salvation, but the Lord still commanded them to "wait for the promise of the Father" (Acts 1:4), speaking of the baptism with the Spirit.

Receiving the Power

The Holy Spirit enters our spirits when we are born again. He baptized us into Jesus, but we still need to be baptized with the Spirit by Jesus. I once heard a minister describe the Spirit's presence in salvation as the "Spirit within" because the Spirit enters our spirits when we are born again; this minister describes the baptism with the Spirit as the "Spirit upon" as well. These two phrases have helped me understand the different operations of the Holy Spirit in salvation and when we are baptized with Him.

We have already looked at Acts 1:8, but let's look at it again in light of the minister's description:

But ye shall receive power, after that the Holy Ghost is come upon you: and ye shall be witnesses unto me both in Jerusalem, and in all Judaea, and in Samaria, and unto the uttermost part of the earth.

The verse tells us power is received when the Holy Spirit has come upon us. Jesus said this as well to a group of believers.

The Moment Thomas Confessed Jesus as Lord

I recognize some who read this book may question whether the disciples were saved or not when Jesus addressed them in Acts 1. Let's look at Romans 10:8-9, which provides the criteria for being born again:

But what saith it? The word is nigh thee, even in thy mouth, and in thy heart: that is, the word of faith, which we preach; that if thou shalt confess with thy mouth the Lord Jesus, and shalt believe in thine heart that God hath raised him from the dead, thou shalt be saved.

This verse lists two requirements for a person to be saved: 1) believe in their heart and 2) confess with the mouth the Lord Jesus is their Savior. I have ministered at churches consisting of several denominations and found all agree on this point. Seeing this in the Scriptures, we have already looked at the disciples' experience with Jesus in John 20:22. One disciple, Thomas, was not present and at first rejected the other disciples' accounts of seeing the risen Lord. His attitude changed though when Jesus appeared to him personally:

And after eight days again his disciples were within, and Thomas

with them: then came Jesus, the doors being shut, and stood in the
midst, and said, Peace be unto you. Then saith he to Thomas, Reach
hither thy finger, and behold my hands; and reach hither thy hand,
and thrust it into my side: and be not faithless, but believing. And
Thomas answered and said unto him, MY LORD AND MY GOD.

JOHN 20:26-28

Thomas believed Jesus had been raised from the dead and confessed Him as his Lord; this was the moment he was saved according to the verses we just looked at in Romans 10. I believe we can
conclusively say, with this verse, there is a separate experience after
salvation that the Bible refers to as being baptized with the Spirit.

Drawn by the Spirit to Christ

Some groups within the church believe the disciples were not saved
before the Holy Spirit fell on the day of Pentecost (Acts 2:1-4); others believe we receive Him at salvation. I believe the reason we have
so many disagreements about the Holy Spirit and His operations
in this area is we do not separate the two experiences. This is why
I like the way the minister I referenced earlier described the difference between salvation and being baptized with the Spirit: The Spirit
within and the Spirit upon.

I have had people point to Matthew 10:1 and use it as an argument that the disciples already had the Holy Spirit:

> And when he had called unto him his twelve disciples, he
> gave them power against unclean spirits, to cast them out,
> and to heal all manner of sickness and all manner of disease.

Jesus anointed the disciples and sent them out with the anointing of the Spirit. They were working under the Old Covenant but still healed the sick and cast out demons The Holy Spirit was with them but not in them, so there is a vast difference between Him being with us and in us.

Please do not misunderstand what I am saying. The Holy Spirit works in the lives of both unbelievers and believers. One verse that tells us this in John 6:44:

> No man can come to me, except the Father which hath sent me draw him: and I will raise him up at the last day.

The Father draws us to salvation through the ministry of the Holy Spirit, the foundation of our Christian experience. You cannot be baptized with the Spirit without first receiving Jesus as your Lord.

Baptized by the Spirit into the Body of Christ

The Spirit draws us to salvation and then baptizes us into the body of Christ:

> *For by one Spirit we were all baptized into one body—*
> *whether Jews or Greeks, whether slaves or free—and*
> *have all been made to drink into one Spirit.*
>
> 1 CORINTHIANS 12:13 NKJV

Notice the Holy Spirit is the baptizer when we are saved. We believe in our hearts, confess Jesus as our Lord, and then are baptized by Him into the body of Christ. As we discussed in earlier chapters, the word *baptize* describes the act of immersing. The Spirit literally immerses the new believer into Christ and then seals them with Himself in the Lord's body (Ephesians 1:13).

Baptized with the Spirit

It is the Holy Spirit who baptizes a new believer into the body of Christ. This is a different baptism than the one Jesus spoke of in Acts 1:4. Notice the words of John the Baptist in Matthew 3:11:

> I indeed baptize you with water unto repentance. but he that cometh after me is mightier than I, whose shoes I am not worthy to bear: HE SHALL BAPTIZE YOU WITH THE HOLY GHOST, AND WITH FIRE.

John baptized people in water for repentance, while the Holy Spirit baptizes the new believer into the body of Christ for salvation. Jesus then baptizes the believer with the Spirit and endows them with His power. Three distinct baptisms with three distinct purposes.

Chapter 19

Philip's Ministry in Samaria

*Now when all the people were baptized, it came to pass, that
Jesus also being baptized, and praying, the heaven was opened,
and the Holy Ghost descended in a bodily shape like a dove
upon him, and a voice came from heaven, which said, Thou
art my beloved Son; in thee I am well pleased. And Jesus
himself began to be about thirty years of age, being (as was
supposed) the son of Joseph, which was the son of Heli.*

LUKE 3:21-23

Jesus did not begin His ministry before the Holy Spirit came upon Him when He was baptized by John. The first mention of power in Jesus' life is made in Luke 4:14-15, when He returned from the desert temptations (Luke 4:1-14). If the Lord could not begin His ministry before being baptized with the Spirit, I believe we should not either. This is the reason Jesus commanded His disciples to wait in Jerusalem until they were baptized with the Spirit before launching out as His witnesses (Acts 1:4-5).

The Holy Spirit's Arrival on Pentecost

The disciples waited in the upper room for the promise Jesus told them was coming. As we have already seen, they were already born again while sitting in that room waiting for the Holy Spirit. The Spirit's arrival on Pentecost is recorded in Acts 2:1-4:

> And when the day of Pentecost was fully come, they were all with one accord in one place. And suddenly there came a sound from heaven as of a rushing mighty wind, and it filled all the house where they were sitting. And there appeared unto them cloven tongues like as of fire, and it sat upon each of them. And they were all filled with the Holy Ghost, and began to speak with other tongues, as the Spirit gave them utterance.

The disciples were baptized and filled with the Spirit, and they all "began to speak with other tongues, as the Spirit gave them utterance." There is a lot of confusion in the church today about the gift of tongues. We will examine it in detail later in the book, but let's first look at some other examples of the Spirit coming upon believers.

Philip's Ministry in Samaria

Philip was appointed by the apostles as one of seven men chosen to oversee the early church's daily business. The qualifications for their choice were that each one selected was expected to be "of good reputation, full of the Holy Spirit and wisdom" (Acts 6:3, NKJV). This is a much smaller list than what is often used today. I've seen qualifications such as a clean drug test or criminal record, but rarely have I heard of people selected for being full of the Holy Spirit and God's wisdom.

In the eighth chapter of Acts is the account of Philip preaching in Samaria:

Then Philip went down to the city of Samaria, and preached Christ
unto them. And the people with one accord gave heed unto those
things which Philip spake, hearing and seeing the miracles which he
did. For unclean spirits, crying with loud voice, came out of many
that were possessed with them: and many taken with palsies, and
that were lame, were healed. And there was great joy in that city.

ACTS 8:5-8

The people were attracted to the ministry of Philip for more than just his oratorial skills. They heard his message and saw "the miracles which he did," his ministry a witness to the power of the Spirit. The reason revival came to Samaria and the entire city turned to the Lord was they not only heard the Word of God preached but also saw it confirmed with signs. I believe one of the reasons the church doesn't have a greater impact on the world around us today is because we are not preaching the same message the early church preached to everyone.

Is the Church Still Relevant?

There are many people who have basically written the church off as being irrelevant to the modern era. These people primarily preach the Gospel as a message focused on heaven and hell, leaving all other benefits of our redemption for when we arrive in heaven. I've met many people who love God but have given up on any level of expectation for Him to help them with the struggles experienced in their daily lives.

Can you imagine what would happen if the church could begin to start giving witness of God's Word with signs and wonders to where people's bodies were being healed, marriages supernaturally restored, and financial lack miraculously reversed? People would see the relevance of God in their everyday lives and experience His love firsthand. Unfortunately, this is not happening because such a large portion of the church has chosen to eliminate the baptism of the Spirit and His supernatural operations and gifts.

Philip preached the Gospel, and we see in verse 7 that unclean spirits were cast out, paralytics were healed, and many other forms of miracles manifested. The people responded with great joy and turned to God, confessing Jesus as Lord. I believe this is a model for how ministry should be conducted. How many of us go into a city, preach the Gospel, and expect to see demons cast out and miracles manifest? This is a much better model than the so-called seeker-friendly gospel so many of our churches pursue today.

We Need the Supernatural

Unfortunately, I have been criticized for my focus on the miraculous, as critics have said it takes away from the message of salvation. While I agree our goal is to bring people to a saving knowledge of Christ, I also think the early church used the miraculous to bring people to the Lord. For those who disagree, I point you to Hebrews 2:2-4:

> For if the word spoken by angels was stedfast, and every transgression and disobedience received a just recompence of reward; how shall we escape, if we neglect so great salvation; which at the first began to be spoken by the Lord, and was confirmed unto us by them that heard him; GOD ALSO BEARING THEM WITNESS, BOTH WITH SIGNS AND WONDERS, AND WITH DIVERS MIRACLES, AND GIFTS OF THE HOLY GHOST, according to his own will?

God confirmed Jesus' ministry with "signs and wonders, with various miracles, and gifts of the Holy Spirit." Mark 16:20 tells us Jesus did the same for the early church. I cannot agree with anyone who argues against miracles because in doing so, they inadvertently claim we have grown beyond the level of the Lord and the early church. Neither Jesus nor the early church were able to reach that place, and I do not believe any of us will ever reach that point. In my opinion, it would be prideful to think otherwise.

Drawn by the Spirit's Gifts

Philip used the gifts of the Spirit to draw people to Christ and minister to their needs. He preached, ministered in the power of the Spirit, and then baptized the people:

> *But when they believed Philip preaching the things*
> *concerning the kingdom of God, and the name of Jesus*
> *Christ, they were baptized, both men and women.*
>
> ACTS 8:12

We assume the people were baptized in water based on Acts 8:36-39, where we find Philip baptized an Ethiopian eunuch in water. His only condition is listed in verse 37: "If you believe with all your heart, you may" (NKJV). He was only willing to baptize those who believed "with all [their] heart."

The people in Samaria turned to the Lord and were baptized in water. They were now saved but not baptized with the Spirit. For those who argue against the second experience with the Spirit, notice what the church leadership in Jerusalem did when they heard of the revival happening in Samaria:

Now when the apostles which were at Jerusalem heard that Samaria
had received the word of God, they sent unto them Peter and John:
who, when they were come down, prayed for them, that they might
receive the Holy Ghost: (For as yet he was fallen upon none of
them: only they were baptized in the name of the Lord Jesus.) Then
laid they their hands on them, and they received the Holy Ghost.

ACTS 8:14-17

Peter and John were sent to minister the Holy Spirit to those who had been born again because of Philip's ministry. This shows the importance placed on the baptism with the Spirit.

We Need the Baptism with the Spirit

There was a sorcerer in Samaria who turned to the Lord after seeing the miraculous demonstrations of power occurring in Philip's ministry. I acknowledge Acts 8 does not specifically mention the new believers praying in tongues when Peter and John laid hands on them. It does tell us they did receive the Holy Spirit, and that Simon "saw" the Spirit came upon them when hands were laid on them. This tells us there had to be some form of manifestation following the Spirit coming upon them. Based on the disciples speaking in tongues when they were baptized with the Spirit, I feel it is a safe assumption that is what Simon saw.

Simon saw something that verified the Spirit came upon the new believers in Samaria, the second occurrence in which believers received the experience after their conversion. The first occurred on Pentecost when the Spirit descended on the disciples, who we have already seen were born again when Jesus breathed the Spirit into their spirits, just after His resurrection. In a sense, we could also look at the Lord's life and ministry as the first occurrence.

Jesus was conceived of the Spirit in Mary's womb. He was God in the flesh, but His birth still required the involvement of the Spirit to occur. Luke 1:35 tells us the Holy Spirit came on Mary, and then the power of God "overshadowed" her. The Lord was born of the Spirit and had access to the Holy Spirit as He grew into manhood. The Spirit was with Jesus, but there is not one recorded miracle until after He was baptized with the Spirit, after His baptism in water by John the Baptist.

I am not saying Jesus was not God in the flesh prior to His baptism or that He was less than He should have been. Instead, my goal is to emphasize the importance of the baptism with the Spirit. If Jesus did not begin His ministry without the Spirit's baptism, who are we to think we can have a successful ministry or Christian life without it as well?

Chapter 20

Paul's Ministry in Ephesus

And it came to pass, that, while Apollos was at Corinth, Paul
having passed through the upper coasts came to Ephesus: and
finding certain disciples, he said unto them, Have ye received
the Holy Ghost since ye believed? And they said unto him, We
have not so much as heard whether there be any Holy Ghost.

ACTS 19:1-2

I have spent some discussing the new birth and baptism with the Spirit over the years. The disciples were born again just after the Lord's resurrection and then baptized on the day of Pentecost. We looked in Acts 8 at Philip's ministry in the last chapter and saw those converted during his ministry were baptized with the Holy Spirit as a separate experience just like the disciples. The chapter ended with a brief reference to the fact that Jesus was born of the Spirit but then waited until the Spirit came upon Him when He was baptized in the river Jordan before launching into ministry.

The Spirit and His Anointing

Jesus is a member of the Trinity but still depended on the Spirit in His ministry. The Holy Spirit was in Him from birth but then came upon Him at the point God anointed Him, as described in Acts 10:38:

131

How GOD ANOINTED JESUS OF NAZARETH
WITH THE HOLY GHOST AND WITH POWER:
who went about doing good, and healing all that were
oppressed of the devil; for God was with him.

There is a vast difference between having the Holy Spirit in our
born-again spirit and having Him come upon us with His anointing.
Far too many Christians I've met over the years do not understand
the difference. The Christians understood He filled them when they
were born again but have never been anointed with power because
they have been incorrectly taught about the baptism with the Spirit.

Apollos Sets the Stage for Paul in Ephesus

Let's look at another example of the two experiences in Acts 19 from
Paul's ministry to a group of Ephesian believers. The precursor to his
arrival in Ephesus was the ministry of a Jewish man named Apollos,
who preached Christ in the city without an understanding of anything beyond John's baptism for repentance:

> And a certain Jew named Apollos, born at Alexandria, an eloquent
> man, and mighty in the scriptures, came to Ephesus. This man was
> instructed in the way of the Lord; and being fervent in the spirit, he
> spake and taught diligently the things of the Lord, knowing only
> the baptism of John. And he began to speak boldly in the synagogue:
> whom when Aquila and Priscilla had heard, they took him unto
> them, and expounded unto him the way of God more perfectly.
>
> ACTS 18:24-26

There is no evidence of Apollos being born again or baptized with
the Spirit. He was simply a Jewish man who had been exposed to the

ministry of John the Baptist. Apollos was fervent in serving God but was limited in his revelation. Thankfully, Aquila and Priscilla were able to set him straight.

Paul's Encounter in Ephesus

When Paul arrived in Ephesus, he found a group of believers who had heard Apollos preach the baptism of repentance. The account of his encounter with them is found in Acts 19:1-7:

> And it came to pass, that, while Apollos was at Corinth, Paul having passed through the upper coasts came to Ephesus: and finding certain disciples, he said unto them, HAVE YE RECEIVED THE HOLY GHOST SINCE YE BELIEVED? And they said unto him, We have not so much as heard whether there be any Holy Ghost. And he said unto them, Unto what then were ye baptized? And they said, Unto John's baptism. Then said Paul, John verily baptized with the baptism of repentance, saying unto the people, that they should believe on him which should come after him, that is, on Christ Jesus. When they heard this, they were baptized in the name of the Lord Jesus. And WHEN PAUL HAD LAID HIS HANDS UPON THEM, THE HOLY GHOST CAME ON THEM; and they spake with tongues, and prophesied. And all the men were about twelve.

I find it interesting Paul's first question to the Ephesian believers was, "Did you receive the Holy Spirit when you believed?" How many times have you heard a minister ask a question like this when first meeting someone claiming to be a believer? The men Paul addressed this question to had not heard anything about the Holy Spirit. Their exposure was limited to Apollos's preaching, and so they only knew about "John's baptism."

Paul's encounter with the Ephesian believers proves there is more to be received beyond salvation. He did not know they had not been born again and may even have assumed they had when asking if they had received the Holy Spirit. Apollos had only been exposed to John the Baptist, who first made mention of believers being baptized with the Spirit and fire in Matthew 3:11.

John preached about the coming Messiah and emphasized the need to prepare for His arrival by repenting and being baptized in water; Jesus is the one John the Baptist referred to. There is so much more to salvation provided through the Lord's death, burial, and resurrection than just forgiveness of sins. As commanded by Jesus in Acts 1:4, we must move beyond salvation to the baptism with the Spirit. Being immersed in the Spirit is the point in which we are introduced to the power of God, enabling us to live victoriously.

> *I indeed baptize you with water unto repentance, but*
> *He who is coming after me is mightier than I, whose*
> *sandals I am not worthy to carry. **He will baptize you***
> ***with the Holy Spirit and fire.** (emphasis added)*
>
> MATTHEW 3:11 NKJV

Ephesian Believers Saved and Then Baptized with the Holy Spirit

There are historical records pointing to Apollos being present when John baptized Jesus. It appears he saw the Holy Spirit descending onto Jesus and at once went out, telling everyone he met the Messiah had arrived. The problem with this is Apollos was not a personal follower of Jesus. Like so many new believers today, he was proclaiming a message but lacked revelation knowledge of the things he was proclaiming.

It is obvious from the Ephesians' reaction to Paul's question that Apollos did not preach about the resurrection of Jesus or about being baptized with the Holy Spirit. Paul asked them about their baptism, and they responded that they had been baptized for repentance as taught by John the Baptist. Apollos did not have the full Gospel message because he didn't know about the death and resurrection or about being filled with the Spirit and receiving power from God. Paul shared the full message with them, as shown in Acts 19:4-6:

> Then said Paul, John verily baptized with the baptism of repentance, saying unto the people, that they should believe on him which should come after him, that is, on Christ Jesus. When they heard this, they were baptized in the name of the Lord Jesus. And when Paul had laid his hands upon them, the Holy Ghost came on them; and they spake with tongues, and prophesied.

The Ephesian believers listened to Paul, were born again, and then "baptized in the name of the Lord Jesus." Notice, Paul was not satisfied with the conversion as most of us would be today. He laid his hands on the new believers and "Holy Spirit came upon them," and then these new believers spoke in tongues just as the believers did on the day of Pentecost and in Samaria. Once again, we see a group of people who believed in Jesus and had been born again being baptized with the Holy Spirit after their conversion.

Chapter 21

Should All Believers Speak in Tongues?

*But God hath chosen the foolish things of the world to confound
the wise; and God hath chosen the weak things of the world
to confound the things which are mighty; and base things of
the world, and things which are despised, hath God chosen,
yea, and things which are not, to bring to nought things that
are: that no flesh should glory in his presence. But of him are
ye in Christ Jesus, who of God is made unto us wisdom, and
righteousness, and sanctification, and redemption: that, according
as it is written, He that glorieth, let him glory in the Lord.*

1 CORINTHIANS 1:27-31

The baptism with the Spirit is not more important than being born again as some claim. At the same time, it is not possible to release what was put in our spirits at salvation without it. We have spent some time in the earlier chapters discussing the baptism and have shown conclusively it is a separate experience available to those who have been born again. A gift of the Spirit seen in Scripture, accompanying being baptized with the Spirit, is speaking in tongues. In this chapter, we will look in the Word of God with a goal of finding out whether this gift is or is not for all believers and relevant for us today.

The Carnality of the Corinthians

The Corinthian church was filled with carnality when Paul wrote his letters to it. There was incest commonly reported that was not dealt with. Groups within it were even getting drunk when they took communion. Terrible things were happening. There were also excesses throughout the church, and people were standing up interrupting the flow of worship to speak in tongues constantly throughout the meetings being held. Paul set restrictions in his letters for public assemblies, such as saying that only two, or at the most three, people speak in tongues, and only if there was an accompanying interpretation.

The group of people who operated in the gifts of the Spirit were carnal and had no understanding of the Holy Spirit as anything more than something manifesting in the meetings. They were immature and clueless about the relationship available to them with the Spirit. I believe we can safely say they were the most carnal church Paul ever wrote to. They were excessive and controlled by their emotions and physical senses instead of the Spirit of God.

Restrictions Were Not Prohibitions

Paul put restrictions on how the gifts of the Spirit should be used in his letters to the churches but did not say they should cease to function. An example of this is seen in 1 Corinthians 14:39:

> Wherefore, brethren, covet to prophesy, and forbid not
> to speak with tongues.

There were a lot of things the Corinthian believers were doing that were wrong. Paul called these behaviors out in his two letters, but he also provided corrections. The translated word "desire" in this verse describes having an exceedingly strong desire to prophecy and is often translated as "lust" in many modern translations. We are to earnestly desire prophecy in public meetings but should not forbid speaking in tongues. Both were to be done in moderation, as they are vital operations of the Holy Spirit.

I have heard ministers use the book of Corinthians to argue against the gifts and operations of the Spirit. The common argument is they were the source of all carnal practices in that church. This is equivalent to saying that extending an invitation to the Holy Spirit in our services opens the door to carnality among our congregations! This is obviously nonsense and has served to rob many wonderful people of experiencing Him in any form.

Is the Love of God Superior to the Spirit's Gifts?

The apostle Paul acknowledged carnality but never told a single person to quit operating in the gifts of the Spirit. Instead, he told them to do it properly, providing a list of the nine gifts in 1 Corinthians 12 and then discussing them in chapters 12-14. Chapter 13 is focused on the love of God, which is the foundation on which our ability to work in the gifts of the Spirit is built.

I have heard people say the love of God supersedes our need for the gifts, often using 1 Corinthians 12:27-31 to justify their argument:

> Now ye are the body of Christ, and members in particular. And God hath set some in the church, first apostles, secondarily prophets, thirdly teachers, after that miracles,

then gifts of healings, helps, governments, diversities of tongues. Are all apostles? are all prophets? are all teachers? are all workers of miracles? Have all the gifts of healing? do all speak with tongues? do all interpret? But covet earnestly the best gifts: and yet shew I unto you a more excellent way.

Some ministers use these verses as proof love is the "more excellent way" than the gifts of the Spirit. I had several professors in Bible college who followed this train of thought. It did not bear witness within my spirit, but I did not have enough information to refute what I was hearing in class.

I spent some time with the Holy Spirit discussing the things I was hearing in class. One day He asked me if I knew what the "excellent way" Paul wrote about was. Some say it is love alone, but the Holy Spirit showed me it was something different. Taking into context with the whole book of Corinthians, we see he was saying the gifts working by and through love are superior to them working for selfish purposes. We see then love does not supersede the Holy Spirit's gifts and manifestations but instead is the foundation from which they flow.

Sounding Brass and Tinkling Cymbals

The thirteenth chapter of 1 Corinthians is known as the Love Chapter, beginning with an interesting statement about speaking in tongues that is often misunderstood:

> *Though I speak with the tongues of men and of angels, and have not charity, I am become as sounding brass, or a tinkling cymbal.*

1 CORINTHIANS 13:1

I have heard this verse used to support arguments against speaking in tongues, but Paul was not telling his readers they should not exercise this gift. Instead, he was telling them it would not help them if exercised outside of God's love. As mentioned previously, love is the foundation on which our individual Christian journey is built. This is seen in 1 Corinthians 13:2-3:

> And though I have the gift of prophecy, and understand all
> mysteries, and all knowledge; and though I have all faith,
> so that I could remove mountains, and have not charity,
> I am nothing. And though I bestow all my goods to feed
> the poor, and though I give my body to be burned, and
> have not charity, it profiteth me nothing.

I have heard arguments using these verses against tongues being a valid gift. Notice that Paul also mentioned prophecy, mysteries, all knowledge, and faith, in addition to the gift of tongues. Have you ever heard anyone argue these are not for us today?

Speaking in tongues is a valid gift available to every believer like any other gift of the Spirit. The arguments against it are largely a result of well-meaning people trying to interpret Scripture using their reason instead of looking to the Holy Spirit for answers. He showed me years ago that reason is the fruit of self-effort, while revelation is the fruit of relationship with Him. You will struggle with developing a relationship unless you first understand your identity in Christ Jesus and acknowledge the Spirit's presence within your born-again spirit.

Chapter 22

God's Love Is
Our Foundation

Though I speak with the tongues of men and of angels, and have not
charity, I am become as sounding brass, or a tinkling cymbal. And
though I have the gift of prophecy, and understand all mysteries, and
all knowledge; and though I have all faith, so that I could remove
mountains, and have not charity, I am nothing. And though I
bestow all my goods to feed the poor, and though I give my body
to be burned, and have not charity, it profiteth me nothing.

1 CORINTHIANS 13:1-3

We finished the last chapter with these verses from 1 Corinthians, often used by critics of the baptism with the Spirit
as proof that it is not a valid experience for today. The problem with
this argument is it only pulls out the gift of tongues, ignoring Paul's
reference to other gifts, such as faith, prophecy, etc. It is simply not
possible to use these verses to say the gift of tongues is not valid without saying the other gifts listed are not as well.

Paul is telling us the foundation of all spiritual gifts is love. A person operating in the gifts of the Spirit who is not walking in love
is just making noise. Love is our foundation, and it must be the

motivation for all we do in our Christian walks. There are many references to Jesus being "moved with compassion," such as stated in Matthew 14:14:

> And Jesus went forth, and saw a great multitude, and was moved with compassion toward them, and he healed their sick.

The phrase "was moved with compassion" is translated from the Greek word *splagchnizomai,* which portrays Jesus being deeply moved from His inner being, where the Holy Spirit lives; He is within our born-again spirit just as He was with the Lord. Many people express the desire to minister as Jesus did, and this is something we should all aspire to. Achieving this ability will require us to cultivate a relationship with the Spirit and reach a point of complete dependence on Him.

Love Is the Foundation

John 4:12-16 offers further insight into the love of God present in every Christian's spirit:

> Art thou greater than our father Jacob, which gave us the well, and drank thereof himself, and his children, and his cattle? Jesus answered and said unto her, Whosoever drinketh of this water shall thirst again: but whosoever drinketh of the water that I shall give him shall never thirst; but the water that I shall give him shall be in him a well of water springing up into everlasting life. The woman saith unto him, Sir, give me this water, that I thirst not, neither come hither to draw. Jesus saith unto her, Go, call thy husband, and come hither.

Notice the phrase "born of God"; this reminds us of Jesus' conversation with Nicodemus, found in John 3:3-8:

> Jesus answered and said unto him, Verily, verily, I say unto thee, EXCEPT A MAN BE BORN AGAIN, he cannot see the kingdom of God. Nicodemus saith unto him, How can a man be born when he is old? can he enter the second time into his mother's womb, and be born? Jesus answered, Verily, verily, I say unto thee, EXCEPT A MAN BE BORN OF WATER AND OF THE SPIRIT, he cannot enter into the kingdom of God. That which is born of the flesh is flesh; and that which is BORN OF THE SPIRIT is spirit. Marvel not that I said unto thee, YE MUST BE BORN AGAIN. The wind bloweth where it listeth, and thou hearest the sound thereof, but canst not tell whence it cometh, and whither it goeth: so is every one that is BORN OF THE SPIRIT.

The phrases "born of God" and "born of the Spirit" both refer to being born again. Since God is love, we could say that those who have been born again have been "born of love." Paul tells us that the "love of God has been poured out in our hearts by the Holy Spirit" (Romans 5:5, NKJV); this happened the moment we confessed Jesus as our Lord and were born again.

Do We Still Need the Spirit and His Gifts?

Love is the fundamental, spiritual nature of every Christian. This is the reason I said previously that it is not possible to develop a relationship with the Spirit if you are not walking in love. God is love, the Holy Spirit is love, and every born-again Christian is filled with love. Love will always be the foundation on which our relationship with the Spirit is built, as our ability to operate in His gifts flows from this relationship. I have seen that the people who have the greatest moves of the Spirit in their ministries are those who have developed an intimate relationship with the Spirit of God.

The gifts of the Spirit are valid for us today just as they were for Jesus and His disciples in their ministries. I have spent some time, starting in the last chapter, talking about this because so many people struggle with the ministry of the Holy Spirit. Most of them have been exposed to wrong teaching, often focused more on manifestations or emotional experiences rather than on developing a relationship with the Spirit. The baptism with the Spirit is our entrance into His anointing, but it is also our entrance into a relationship that is far too often neglected in the church today.

I grew up in a church that did not believe in the baptism of the Spirit or His gifts. Our pastor told us anyone who spoke in tongues was yielding to Satan. He was wrong; his ministry focused on forgiveness of sins, but I do not recall there ever being any mention in his ministry of God's willingness to accept me as I was or to fill me with His Spirit. If you asked our pastor about the miracles that happened in the Bible, speaking in tongues, or prophecy, he would say they were not for us today. I heard him say this many times but cannot recall him every offering an explanation for why he believed the gifts were no longer needed.

Has the Perfect Come?

I have heard people using 1 Corinthians 13:8-10 to argue against the validity of tongues for believers today:

Charity never faileth: but whether there be prophecies, they shall fail; whether there be tongues, they shall cease; whether there be knowledge, it shall vanish away. For we know in part, and we prophesy in part. But when that which is perfect is come, then that which is in part shall be done away.

I have met people who interpret these verses and claim they are referring to the Bible. They argue that the early church needed the gifts of the Spirit because the written Word of God had not been completed. It seemed like they believed that we no longer need the Holy Spirit today because "that which is perfect has come." Some teach that we no longer need signs, wonders, and miracles because we have the Bible today. The issue with their reasoning is that the context in which these verses were written has nothing to do with the completion of Scripture.

The Bible is a flawless representation of the Word of God, free of error. I strongly believe in the infallibility of Scripture. I am passionate about the Word, but that is not the perfect thing Paul was referring to in 1 Corinthians 13. We can see this in 1 Corinthians 13:11-12:

When I was a child, I spake as a child, I understood as a child, I thought as a child: but when I became a man, I put away childish things. For now we see through a glass, darkly; but then face to face: now I know in part; but then shall I know even as also I am known.

Let's consider a couple of questions based on these verses. Firstly, have we seen Jesus "face to face"? Secondly, do we have a complete understanding of all things as God does yet? The answer to both questions is no, which means that the "that which is perfect" Paul is referring to has not yet occurred.

The Glorified Body

If the "perfect" Paul was referring to has not yet come, we need to ask what it was then. Paul was speaking of the glorified body that all believers will receive when the Lord returns for His bride. At that time, we will no longer need to operate in the gifts of the Spirit or speak in tongues; the spiritual manifestations and operations of the Holy Spirit are meant for the church to use in this age. They will not be needed once we have received our full redemption in all three realms: spirit, soul, and body.

When we receive our glorified bodies, we will not need the gifts of the Spirit because we will be in complete union, fellowship, and communion with God. There will be no inadequacies to deal with anymore. Let me share another passage of Scripture in Romans 8:26:

> Likewise the Spirit also helpeth our infirmities: for we know not what we should pray for as we ought: but the Spirit itself maketh intercession for us with groanings which cannot be uttered.

The abovementioned verse is speaking of the help available to all believers who will look to the Holy Spirit and allow Him to partner with them. Notice, Paul tells us the Spirit will help us with "groanings which cannot be uttered," which fits in perfectly with our discussion in 1 Corinthians 13.

The "weaknesses" Paul is speaking of is not necessarily sickness, as many may think. It could be a reference to sickness, but in context the word is speaking of inadequacies of any kind. Not knowing how to pray is an inadequacy every Christian experiences. The Holy Spirit will partner with us in prayer and provide utterance to speak directly from our born-again spirits. There are many other areas He will help us with that we will look at in later chapters.

Chapter 23

Be Being Filled with the Spirit

*And be not drunk with wine, wherein is
excess; but be filled with the Spirit.*

EPHESIANS 5:18

It often seems like many people believe speaking in tongues is a way to demonstrate that we have been baptized with the Holy Spirit. While our prayer language is indeed evidence of being baptized with the Spirit, the gift encompasses more than just that and is not the sole indicator of having been baptized with the Spirit.

One cannot speak in tongues without first being baptized with the Spirit, which is why the gift is considered as proof that the baptism happened. I once watched a video from the 1960s while I was attending Bible school in the early 1990s of a Full Gospel Businessmen's meeting in which a leading healing evangelist of the day, Kathryn Kuhlman, spoke. Ms. Kuhlman was upset with the ministers in the meeting due to the amount of time spent on preliminaries, announcements, and mutual admiration.

Continuous Fillings

Ms. Kuhlman asked the ministers to raise their hands if they had been baptized with the Holy Ghost. The majority responded and raised their hands as she requested. She then said, "You may have been baptized but have not been filled a single day since." Ms. Kuhlman then went on to explain how the infilling of the Spirit is not a one-time experience, as we are to be continuously filled with the Spirit.

The baptism with the Holy Spirit is not just an experience given to prove God did something in our lives. It is the entrance into a fantastic relationship almost impossible to describe. As we saw in the early chapters, we are filled with the Spirit at salvation, the baptism taking us into a deeper level of experience with Him. As we progress in our Christian journey, there will be many more fillings of His presence in our lives.

The Benefits of Speaking in Tongues

The gift of speaking in tongues has many benefits that are often overlooked by many Christians. I have heard numerous sermons that focus on tongues as evidence of being baptized, without mentioning any other benefits. Many people respond to these messages, exercising their faith and speaking in tongues when they are baptized, but then they never speak in their prayer language again. Some may pray in tongues only during church services and rarely do so in their private prayer times.

I have met people who prayed in tongues once but haven't done so again, even months or years after being baptized with the Spirit. The lack of teaching often leads them to not pursue the gift, and they identify as being Spirit-filled without any evidence. Their claim is usually based on a single moment in time, either while receiving prayer at church or in some other setting.

It's important to note that Jesus does not baptize anyone just to give them a single instant experience that changes everything. The baptism is just the beginning of our journey into deeper spiritual realms where intimacy with the Holy Spirit is found, a truth that the devil does not want any Christian to discover. While the baptism with the Holy Spirit does not guarantee that a person will enter relationship, spiritual maturity, or receive a greater anointing, it does open the door to these experiences.

Continuously Filled with the Spirit

I believe that being baptized with the Spirit is not optional. Jesus' last command to His disciples (Acts 1:4) was to wait for this experience. It is the key to being continuously filled with the Spirit, which is the experience Paul refers to in Ephesians 5:18:

> And be not drunk with wine, wherein is excess; but be filled with the Spirit.

Paul commands his readers to not "be drunk with wine." Do you believe this applies to all Christians? If so, then do you also think his command to "be filled with the Spirit" would also apply equally to all believers? The answer to both questions is "Yes." We are not to be "drunk with wine," and we are to be "filled with the Spirit." God never indented for us to live the Christian life independent of the Holy Spirit.

Dependent on the Spirit

Paul tells us that those who are led by the Spirit of God are the sons of God. The word translated "son" describes a person who shares the same nature as their heavenly Father. Every Christian has a new spirit (2 Corinthians 5:17) that enables them to not only receive the Holy Spirit, but also to be baptized with His presence and enter an intimate relationship with their creator.

You will find your dependence on God grow in relationship to the growth of your relationship with the Holy Spirit. Paul describes the Christian journey in Galatians 2:20:

> I am crucified with Christ: nevertheless I live; yet not I, but Christ liveth in me: and the life which I now live in the flesh I live by the faith of the Son of God, who loved me, and gave himself for me.

Paul is sharing in this verse that his life was lived in complete dependence on Christ. He got to a point where it was no longer about him living his own life but rather about the Holy Spirit enabling Jesus to live through him. Even though Jesus was a part of the Divine Trinity, He still didn't act independently of the Father or the Holy Spirit. I won't get into why this is the case, but simply put, the Father, Son, and Holy Spirit never operate independently of each other.

Unity with the Spirit

When Jesus said He could "do nothing" of Himself (John 5:30), He was referring to the unity of the Divine Trinity. Some people misinterpret His statement to try and discredit His deity, but they fail to understand that the statement was a reference to the Lord's deity. He operated in complete oneness with God, making it impossible for Him to act without the involvement of God or the Holy Spirit. They worked together, and Jesus flowed in complete unity with the Spirit in His life and ministry.

The Father, Son, and Holy Spirit all operate as one and do not act independently from each other. God does not want any of us to operate independently of Him; He wants us to depend on Him just as much as Jesus did. This reliance happens through the ministry of the Holy Spirit, and our dependence on the Father grows as our relationship with the Spirit grows.

Every miracle performed in Jesus' ministry was a manifestation of the Holy Spirit's power. We see an example of this in Luke 5:17:

> And it came to pass on a certain day, as he was teaching, that there were Pharisees and doctors of the law sitting by, which were come out of every town of Galilee, and Judaea, and Jerusalem: and THE POWER OF THE LORD WAS PRESENT TO HEAL THEM.

The power was present because the Holy Spirit was always present with Jesus, as He never ministered without the Holy Spirit. Can we say the same about ourselves when we minister to others? The same Holy Spirit who anointed Jesus is waiting to anoint us today. He lives in the spirit of every born-again Christian and is only waiting for us to acknowledge Him and desires to fill us with a fresh filling of His presence every day.

THE LANGUAGE OF THE SPIRIT

And they were all filled with the Holy Ghost and began to speak with other tongues, as the Spirit gave them utterance.

ACTS 2:4

Chapter 24

A New Tongue

And they were all filled with the Holy Ghost, and began to
speak with other tongues, as the Spirit gave them utterance.

ACTS 2:4

One of the first signs of the Holy Spirit's presence following baptism is the ability to speak in tongues. There are many critics of this practice, but most of them simply lack a proper understanding of the gift due to inadequate teaching. However, incorrect teaching is not limited to those who oppose the gift. Many in Charismatic, Pentecostal, or Word of Faith churches have also not been taught correctly and thus often misrepresent the gift as a result.

One often overlooked truth regarding being baptized with the Spirit is that speaking in tongues is only one aspect of the experience. I've heard many ministers claim that a person cannot be baptized with the Spirit or operate in His gifts without speaking in tongues. While I believe that God desires all baptized individuals to speak in tongues, there are some who may not do so immediately, even though they have the ability. This truth puzzled me when I first encountered it.

They Spoke with Other Tongues

After I was baptized with the Spirit, the most significant change for me was that the Word of God came alive. The Holy Spirit became real and started to reveal things to me from the Word of God. Although I spoke in tongues at my baptism, I did not continue to speak because I was told that the Spirit would speak through me. Over time, I came to understand that although He required my cooperation, the Holy Spirit will never make us open our mouths and speak. We are not puppets, and He will not force us to speak.

Acts 2:4 tells us that "they were all filled with the Holy Spirit and began to speak with other tongues, as the Spirit gave them utterance" (NKJV). He did not speak through them; they had to open their mouths and speak just as we do today. This lack of understanding regarding the responsibility to speak often inhibits people from exercising the gift of tongues, as they wait for the Holy Spirit to speak through them.

I have found the perception that the Holy Spirit will take control and speak through us to be the number one hindrance to people being able to exercise the gift of tongues. Consider 1 Corinthians 14:32, which tells us the "spirits of the prophets are subject to the prophets." I recognize this verse is focused on prophecy and not tongues. Notice, though, that it tells us exercising the gift of prophecy is in the control of the person exercising the gift. In other words, the person must open their mouths to release a prophecy. The Holy Spirit will not force us to prophesy or to speak in tongues.

We Must Cooperate
with the Holy Spirit

I understand that some people who have been baptized with the Spirit may not have spoken in tongues when worshipping the Lord. This may be a controversial statement for some, but I believe it to be true.

While it may be due to wrong teaching, it's important to acknowledge that the Holy Spirit works through our misunderstandings and traditions as best as possible. Operating in any gift of the Spirit requires our cooperation and willingness to do our part.

In my experience, when leading people into the baptism with the Holy Spirit, I've observed that the individual being ministered to must exercise their faith. The Spirit does not force anything upon us, and a person is never baptized with the Spirit against their will. Similarly, speaking in tongues also requires us to open our mouths and speak, even after being baptized with the Holy Spirit.

I do believe it is possible to receive the baptism with the Holy Spirit and not speak in tongues. However, this is not because it is God's will but rather because of His mercy and willingness to provide what is asked for. Unfortunately, many Christians may unknowingly resist the Holy Spirit and His gifts due to being misinformed. Any person who understands the Scriptures' teachings about being baptized with the Holy Spirit and willingly rejects speaking in tongues or experiencing other spiritual gifts may not have been baptized properly and could be at risk spiritually.

The Gifts of the Spirit

Speaking in tongues is one gift of the Spirit we gain access to through the baptism with the Spirit. We see a list of these gifts in 1 Corinthians 12:7-11 and Romans 12:7-8, and then are told in 1 Corinthians 12 the foundation on which all operate is the love of God. Love is the foundation, but there is a caveat you need to be aware of. It is possible to operate in the gifts of the Spirit but still be carnal. This is proven by the people in the Corinthian church Paul was writing to. Those people were carnal, and a large part of the Corinthian letters from Paul focused on correcting their misuse of spiritual gifts.

If you have ever been in a so-called Pentecostal service, you've seen people who have misused spiritual gifts. This does not happen in every service, but you will see this if you attend enough services; people who will stand up and gift a message in tongues or offer a prophecy with a totally wrong motive. They are not standing up to be a blessing but instead, in most cases, to make themselves look spiritual in the eyes of their fellow congregants.

Carnality and the Gifts of the Spirit

Many people I've met disagree with this belief about being both carnal and speaking in tongues, so this idea requires further consideration. A common belief taught today is that a person must be a hundred percent spiritual person for the Holy Spirit to use them to manifest His gifts. We will discuss operating in the gifts and come back to this idea later; for now, it's something you should be aware of for the present time.

There are many misunderstandings about the Spirit, His gifts, and how they work. In 1 Corinthians 13, we learn that the gifts operating in the love of God will always be better than the gifts operating through our carnality. Chapter 14 provides insight into the gifts of prophecy and speaking in tongues, which Paul gives qualifications and instructions for exercising them. Notice 1 Corinthians 14:1-2:

> Follow after charity, and desire spiritual gifts, but rather that ye may prophesy. For he that speaketh in an unknown tongue speaketh not unto men, but unto God: for no man understandeth him; howbeit in the spirit he speaketh mysteries.

In the upcoming chapter, we will delve into the topics of tongues and prophecy in depth. However, there is one final issue that needs to be addressed. Many believe that speaking in tongues is a valid gift for the church today but do not necessarily believe every believer will receive it. While it is believed that everyone has the potential to speak in tongues, not everyone will. This discrepancy is mainly due to our current misunderstanding of spiritual matters. Through the content shared in this book, I pray that your spiritual eyes will be opened to the ministry of the Holy Spirit and His wonderful presence in your life.

Chapter 25

Benefits of Praying in Tongues

*And these signs shall follow them that believe; In my name shall they
cast out devils; THEY SHALL SPEAK WITH NEW TONGUES;
they shall take up serpents; and if they drink any deadly thing, it shall
not hurt them; they shall lay hands on the sick, and they shall recover.*

MARK 16:17-18

Jesus mentioned the gift of tongues as one of the signs that would
follow those who believe. There is often confusion surrounding
speaking in tongues, not only among those who oppose the gift but
also among individuals who have experienced it after being baptized
with the Spirit. Many such individuals struggle to understand the
purpose of speaking in tongues and may see it as a means to prove
their baptism to others. However, the gift of tongues is much more
than that. It is just one aspect of the experience and serves as a sign
of being baptized with the Spirit.

The Need to Interpret Tongues

I will share insights from the Holy Spirit about speaking in tongues,
beginning with 1 Corinthians 14:1-5:

Follow after charity, and desire spiritual gifts, but rather that ye may prophesy. For he that speaketh in an unknown tongue speaketh not unto men, but unto God: for no man understandeth him; howbeit in the spirit he speaketh mysteries. But he that prophesieth speaketh unto men to edification, and exhortation, and comfort. He that speaketh in an unknown tongue edifieth himself; but he that prophesieth edifieth the church. I would that ye all spake with tongues but rather that ye prophesied: for greater is he that prophesieth than he that speaketh with tongues, except he interpret, that the church may receive edifying.

The first thing we see in these verses is a person who speaks in tongues is speaking directly to God; this is the reason Paul said it is better to prophesy in a public meeting. The Holy Spirit gave a formula to help me understand how the gifts of tongues and prophecy apply in a public meeting:

tongues + interpretation = prophecy

The person speaking in tongues is speaking to God; it will not be understood by anyone else in a public meeting if it is not interpreted. I believe this is the reason Paul encourages every person who prays in tongues to also pray they may interpret. In context, 1 Corinthians is speaking of a public meeting and not our personal prayer lives, but this does not mean we should not seek an interpretation of the things we are praying for.

Prophecy or Tongues?

Paul emphasized the importance of prophecy over speaking in tongues in public, stating that prophesying provides benefit to all present as it is conveyed truth in a known language, while speaking in tongues without interpretation only benefits the speaker. However, he also mentioned that speaking in tongues with interpretation in a public service can be as beneficial as a prophetic utterance.

I have come across various definitions of prophecy, but I have come to understand prophecy as the revelation of God's mysteries in a known language, which is not limited to public gatherings. One can also experience prophetic utterances while praying at home. In 1 Corinthians 14, Paul discussed the exercise of prophecy, tongues, and interpretation of tongues in the context of public meetings. Still, these gifts should also be practiced during private prayer.

Paul also mentioned that he spoke in tongues more than the believers in Corinth (1 Corinthians 14:18), which raises the question of whether he did this during public services or privately. Some ministers argue that he did speak in public, but considering the context of his statement, it seems more likely that he was referring to his private prayer life if he spoke in tongues more than the entire group of believers in Corinth. This suggests that not every born-again, baptized believer filled with the Spirit will publicly exercise the gift of tongues. Most Christians who speak with tongues do so in their private prayer time, as this gift is key to their ability to understand and fellowship with the Holy Spirit.

All Believers Can Speak in Tongues

In 1 Corinthians 12:30, Paul asks whether every believer would speak in tongues:

> Have all the gifts of healing? DO ALL SPEAK WITH TONGUES? do all interpret?

I mentioned this question earlier, but it's essential to address it again. This verse is often misunderstood to mean that the gift of tongues is intended for only some Christians. In its context, Paul's question pertains to public services. The answer to his question is no; only some believers will speak in tongues publicly. However, this does not imply that every Christian cannot speak in tongues privately.

Paul mentioned that he spoke in tongues more than all the Corinthian believers. However, it's essential to note what he said next:

> *I thank my God, I speak with tongues more than ye*
> *all: Yet in the church I had rather speak five words with*
> *my understanding, that by my voice I might teach others*
> *also, than ten thousand words in an unknown tongue.*
>
> 1 CORINTHIANS 14:18-19

There is a vast difference between speaking in tongues privately and in public, something not emphasized enough and that brings a lot of confusion because we have not made a clear distinction about this.

Speaking in Tongues Promotes Spiritual Growth

Speaking in tongues can intentionally promote spiritual growth in our lives.

> *He that speaketh in an unknown tongue edifieth*
> *himself; but he that prophesieth edifieth the church.*
>
> 1 CORINTHIANS 14:4

Every believer can and should speak in tongues; including this practice in your daily Christian life can benefit you by promoting spiritual growth. By spending time praying in tongues, you can edify yourself and develop spiritually. Many Christians who have been baptized with the Spirit are unaware of this simple truth. Speaking in tongues is a way to promote spiritual growth and "[build ourselves] up on [our] most holy faith" (Jude 1:20, NKJV). Modern translations of Jude 1:20 refer to praying in tongues as "praying in the Holy Spirit." I have personally experienced spiritual growth and faith-building when I commit time to praying in tongues as the Spirit gives me utterance, and I believe you will experience the same in your life.

Building Yourself Up in Faith

We can identify two additional benefits of speaking in tongues in Jude 1:20-21:

> But ye, beloved, building up yourselves on your most holy faith, praying in the Holy Ghost, keep yourselves in the love of God, looking for the mercy of our Lord Jesus Christ unto eternal life.

You can "[build yourself up] on your most holy faith" and "keep [yourself] in the love of God" by spending time speaking in tongues. People who discipline themselves to pray in the Spirit in this way will promote spiritual growth, increase their ability to operate in faith, and push themselves into a deeper experience with the love of God. I don't know why anyone would not want to make speaking in tongues a part of their daily spiritual routine!

I was raised in a denominational church that taught against the baptism with the Holy Spirit and the miraculous. Our pastor believed people who operated in these things were yielding to Satan and went so far as to say every person who spoke in tongues was demon-possessed. You may have heard similar statements in your church. Let me ask you a question that helped me in this situation: Would you expect to find people speaking in tongues and performing miracles in a bar or strip club? These places are full of demons, but I've never heard anyone testify to seeing a person healed in them.

The only people I have met over the years who speak in tongues have been born again and baptized with the Spirit. They all love God and desire His presence in their lives. Some have even developed a very intimate relationship with the Holy Spirit and have seen miracles manifesting in their lives. This is a totally different picture than the one presented by the pastor I grew up under. I believe people who oppose those of us who have pressed into the Holy Spirit and His gifts, operations, and manifestations do so only because they have never been taught correctly and see it as harmful.

Chapter 26

My Spirit Prays

For if I pray in an unknown tongue, my spirit
prayeth, but my understanding is unfruitful.

1 CORINTHIANS 14:14

P aul set an example for us to follow when praying in tongues, explaining in 1 Corinthians 14:14 that this type of prayer bypasses our souls and allows us to pray from our born-again spirits. When you pray in tongues, it is not your mind praying. Through this gift, the Holy Spirit enables us to pray directly from our spirit, removing all limitations from our prayer lives. The results may not be immediate when you first start praying in tongues; still, it will significantly accelerate your relationship with the Holy Spirit if you persist and make this practice a part of your daily journey.

Step by Step

It was a huge leap of faith for me to dedicate time to praying in tongues every day. My flesh and soul resisted, as initially, it didn't seem to be yielding any benefits to me. The Holy Spirit directed me to Isaiah 28:10 for my concern:

For precept must be upon precept, precept upon precept;
line upon line, line upon line; here a little, and there a little.

He showed me that spiritual growth is not immediately apparent in the natural realm. There is a process of bringing your flesh into submission to Him. The Holy Spirit showed me through this verse that our spiritual growth occurs line upon line, one step at a time. Praying in tongues acts like a power tool in the natural, enabling you to accelerate the process in ways that cannot be accessed by praying in our known language.

When you first start operating in this gift, there will probably be questions, and you might also have reservations. I did, and I have talked to many others who have had similar experiences. As the benefits are not immediately discernible, you may even question whether this is from God or if it is just you trying to conjure something up. For myself, it took just over a year of praying in tongues every day before I noticed anything discernible in my relationship with the Spirit.

Bypassing Your Brain

Paul tells us in 1 Corinthians 14:14 that when we pray in tongues, it is our spirit praying, not our understanding or intellect. This is why he mentioned that it would be "unfruitful" to pray in tongues without understanding. Speaking in tongues allows us to pray directly from our renewed spirit, bypassing our unrenewed mind, as the Holy Spirit, residing in our spirit, provides the utterance for praying in tongues.

Our minds often have incorrect thinking that needs to be corrected through the Word of God. Renewing our minds takes time (Romans 12:2), and praying only with our intellect can lead to incorrect prayers, limiting our fellowship with the Holy Spirit. However, the gift of tongues removes these limitations by enabling us to pray directly from our spirits.

In 1 Corinthians 2:16, Paul speaks of having the "mind of Christ," referring to our complete spirit. When we pray in the spirit, we use a language not limited by wrong thinking, doctrine, or fear. Speaking in tongues is a powerful way to pray, especially when facing attacks from the enemy, who often uses fear that operates in our soul. Therefore, it is beneficial to bypass our soul and pray directly from our spirit.

Many Christians have faced times of depression or discouragement, both conditions being operations of the soul. Our spirit has never been depressed or discouraged. When you pray in tongues, your spirit is praying out the hidden wisdom of God. The gift of tongues enables us to pray the perfect will of God, which is why it edifies us (1 Corinthians 14:4) and builds us up on our most holy faith (Jude 1:20).

Moving Yourself into a Position of Faith

I once heard Reverend Oral Roberts say that he would only pray for the sick after spending time praying in tongues. He even refused to pray for anyone in English without first praying in the Spirit. This surprised me at first because I did not understand the power of my prayer language. The Holy Spirit helped me understand that Reverend Roberts knew he was building himself up on his most holy faith when he prayed in tongues. His ability to operate in the measure of faith given to him by God (Romans 12:3) increased directly in proportion to the amount of time spent praying in tongues. I have found this to be true in my life as well, and I believe you will too.

Today, many Christians have begun to understand the power of tongues. The Holy Spirit is helping us move out of our carnal traditions into the supernatural realm that all believers should be walking in. He is doing this by teaching us how to function through our new-born spirit instead of our unrenewed souls or five physical senses. I encourage you to set aside time to sit with the Spirit and ask Him to teach you about your spirit if these things are new to you. You will find Him waiting and eager to help.

Also, praying in tongues builds us up. Like Reverend Roberts discovered, it enables us to operate in the highest degree of faith. Those who commit time to this gift each day will find themselves moving into other gifts, such as prophecy and the working of miracles. Speaking in tongues is for much more than just proving you have the Holy Spirit in your life. It puts you into the measure of faith God has given you and will enable you to receive revelation knowledge from the Word of God, flowing in the supernatural power of God.

A Supernatural Rest

Over the years, I've prayed for many people at the altar to be baptized with the Holy Spirit and noticed that many of them start praying in tongues soon after. At first, I was confused by this, but with the help of the Holy Spirit, I came to understand that they were accessing their spirits, which were helping them operate in the faith received from God. Most of them don't even realize that they are being led by the Spirit to build themselves up in faith to operate at their highest potential based on their spiritual growth.

Speaking in tongues helps us to operate in the measure of faith, promotes spiritual growth, and builds us up. It's not just an emotional experience or an outburst of the flesh. According to 1 Corinthians 14:4, speaking in tongues helps us purposefully build ourselves up, leading to an increased awareness of the Holy Spirit's presence. As a result, our relationship with Him will grow, and we will experience a supernatural rest referred to in Isaiah 28:11-12:

For WITH STAMMERING LIPS AND ANOTHER
TONGUE will he speak to this people. To whom he said,
This is the rest wherewith ye may cause the weary to rest;
and this is the refreshing: yet they would not hear.

We know this verse refers to speaking in tongues because Paul
quoted it in 1 Corinthians 14:21:

In the law it is written, With men of other tongues and
other lips will I speak unto this people; and yet for all that
will they not hear me, saith the Lord.

This passage highlights another benefit of speaking in tongues,
emphasizing that speaking in tongues can bring refreshment to the
soul and physical well-being, flowing from the born-again spirit. It
points out that many people today are burdened by stress and pressure, seeking relief through various means such as therapy and herbal
remedies. The passage encourages Christians to recognize that they
have access to a supernatural gift that can provide rest, instead of
pursuing the same solutions as those who do not share their faith.

You do not have to experience stress the way those around you do.
The Holy Spirit resides in your spirit and will partner with you to pray
in tongues at any moment of the day. I have made it a practice to
set aside extra time to do this whenever the demands of work, ministry, and family seem to be getting out of control. Doing so results
in the pressure lifting and provides access to God's wisdom for the
situations I am facing. You can do the exact same thing, as the Holy
Spirit is waiting to help you and only needs your invitation to do so.

Chapter 27

Fluent in the Language of the Spirit

*And I, brethren, when I came to you, came not with excellency
of speech or of wisdom, declaring unto you the testimony of
God. For I determined not to know any thing among you, save
Jesus Christ, and him crucified. And I was with you in weakness,
and in fear, and in much trembling. And my speech and my
preaching was not with enticing words of man's wisdom, but in
demonstration of the Spirit and of power: that your faith should
not stand in the wisdom of men, but in the power of God.*

1 CORINTHIANS 2:1-5

Have you ever wanted to learn a new language? The world seems to be getting smaller, and it seems like those who speak only one language will be limited. Similarly, a Christian who is limited to their natural language will find their ability to access the deeper things of the Spirit limited. They will be able to develop a relationship with the Holy Spirit, but only on a surface level.

In 1 Corinthians 14:4, we have already seen that speaking in tongues enables us to edify ourselves. This basically means that the responsibility for our spiritual growth is in our hands. God has given us the tools, but if we do not utilize them in partnership with the Holy Spirit, we will not grow as He desires for us to. Many people try to develop a relationship with Him using only their souls and five physical senses. While it is possible to have some form of relationship this way, moving into an intimate relationship with God will be impossible.

Praying Mysteries

Many people wonder what their spirits are praying when they speak in their prayer language. This is an important question, and the answer can be found in 1 Corinthians 14:2:

> For he that speaketh in an unknown tongue speaketh not unto men, but unto God: for no man understandeth him; howbeit in the spirit he speaketh mysteries.

When you pray in tongues, you are speaking the hidden mysteries of God. Let me provide some relevant Scriptures for you, starting with 1 Corinthians 2:4:

> And my speech and my preaching was not with enticing words of man's wisdom, but in demonstration of the Spirit and of power.

Paul addressed the strife and division in the Corinthian church in the first chapter of 1 Corinthians, mentioning that the people were relying on their intellect and carnal wisdom. In chapter 2, Paul stated, "When I came to you, [I] did not come with excellence of speech or of wisdom" (NKJV). He wasn't relying on knowledge acquired through study or education, despite being trained in top schools of his day.

Instead, he chose to pray for the wisdom of God. This decision is reflected in his messages and letters, which were filled with the wisdom of God.

The Wisdom of God

Consider Paul's statement in 1 Corinthians 2:6:

> Howbeit we speak wisdom among them that are perfect: yet not the wisdom of this world, nor of the princes of this world, that come to nought.

He was contrasting the wisdom received from times spent praying in tongues and fellowshipping with the Spirit to the wisdom gained through natural means. There is a godly wisdom that is superior to all the knowledge and achievements of man throughout all history. Secular wisdom contradicts the Word of God and will always be inferior to God's wisdom, which was the point Paul makes in 1 Corinthians 2.

Notice the terminology used in 1 Corinthians 2:7:

> But we speak the wisdom of God in a mystery, the hidden wisdom, which God ordained before the ages for our glory. (NKJV)

Paul's messages contained the "wisdom of God in a mystery," which he referred to as "the hidden wisdom." I used to wonder how he was able to access the wisdom if God had hidden it. The Holy Spirit then led me to 1 Corinthians 14:2, which tells us that we "speak mysteries" when we pray in tongues. Paul accessed the "hidden wisdom of God" by spending much time praying in tongues.

Paul's Messages Were
Hard to Understand

Peter was an apostle of Jesus, traveling with the Lord and was personally discipled by Him, along with the other twelve disciples. Notice how he described Paul's messages in 2 Peter 3:14-16:

> Wherefore, beloved, seeing that ye look for such things, be diligent that ye may be found of him in peace, without spot, and blameless. And account that the longsuffering of our Lord is salvation; even as our beloved brother Paul also according to the wisdom given unto him hath written unto you; as also in all his epistles, speaking in them of these things; in which are some things hard to be understood, which they that are unlearned and unstable wrest, as they do also the other scriptures, unto their own destruction.

Paul had a revelation of grace that even astounded the apostles. Where did he get it from? It was certainly not from the teachers in the schools he attended growing up, and he did not learn it as a part of his Jewish training. Galatians 1 provides the answer to how the apostle accessed the wisdom that filled his messages and letters, telling us Paul went into the deserts of Arabia for three years after his encounter with Jesus on the Damascus road.

Paul Accessed God's
Wisdom Praying in Tongues

I believe the Holy Spirit led Paul into the desert. As far as we can tell, he had no contact with any other person for three years. Paul left the desert and traveled to Jerusalem where he spent fifteen days with Peter. He did not receive his revelation during his time with Peter, as it came from his time in the desert with the Bible and praying in tongues.

Paul told the Corinthian believers that he spoke in tongues more then all of them combined (1 Corinthians 14:18). We don't know the exact amount of time Paul spent praying in tongues, but it is obvious from his writings this gift was a central part of his Christian journey. You can access God's hidden wisdom just as Paul did if you commit time each day to spend praying in the Spirit. The gift of speaking in tongues is something we can all exercise at any time in our personal prayer lives.

You need to commit time to praying in tongues in your personal prayer time. At the same time, you should also pray for an interpretation of what is being prayed:

> *Wherefore let him that speaketh in an unknown*
> *tongue pray that he may interpret.*
>
> 1 CORINTHIANS 14:13

You can tap into the wisdom of God at any time. All it takes is a commitment to spend time praying in tongues and then patiently waiting for the interpretation of your prayers from God. It's really that straightforward; the only limitation to this process is your willingness to dedicate yourself to praying. It might sound like I'm simplifying things, but this is the method through which I've received a great deal of insight from the Lord over the years. I simply pray over the Scripture that the Holy Spirit prompts me to and then ask Him for the interpretation. You can also apply this approach in your personal devotional time.

Chapter 28

Drawing on the Wells of Revelation Knowledge

*Even so ye, forasmuch as ye are zealous of spiritual gifts, seek that
ye may excel to the edifying of the church. Wherefore let him that
speaketh in an unknown tongue pray that he may interpret. For if I
pray in an unknown tongue, my spirit prayeth, but my understanding
is unfruitful. What is it then? I will pray with the spirit, and I will
pray with the understanding also: I will sing with the spirit, and I
will sing with the understanding also. Else when thou shalt bless with
the spirit, how shall he that occupieth the room of the unlearned say
Amen at thy giving of thanks, seeing he understandeth not what thou
sayest? For thou verily givest thanks well, but the other is not edified.*

1 CORINTHIANS 14:12-17

Paul referred to the "hidden wisdom of God" in 1 Corinthians
2:6-8 when talking about the content of his sermons. He believed
this wisdom was received from the Holy Spirit while he prayed in
tongues and meditated on Scripture. Most of the fourteenth chapter
of 1 Corinthians addresses the exercise of this gift in public assemblies. Still, it also applies to our personal prayer lives. When we set
aside time to pray in tongues, we are setting aside time to speak the

hidden wisdom of God. It's important to ask the Holy Spirit for an interpretation of what we have been praying for, so that our understanding will benefit from it.

Pray for an Interpretation

Paul tells us to pray for an interpretation whenever someone speaks in tongues during a public meeting. If you pray in tongues during a church service, expect the Holy Spirit to provide an interpretation, blessing everyone present with this knowledge. First Corinthians 14:12-17 applies to public meetings and private prayer lives. Praying in tongues tunes you into the spiritual realm, but without an interpretation, your understanding will not be beneficial.

Interpreting the things prayed out in tongues does not mean you immediately pray out the interpretation in English after praying in tongues. Some people mistakenly do this, but in most cases, the interpretation will come over time in the form of thoughts, ideas, and understanding of Scripture. Sometimes, in our pursuit of the supernatural, we miss the subtle workings of the Spirit because they are not spectacular.

You will not necessarily get a word-for-word interpretation of the things you have been praying in tongues. In my personal life, I ask the Holy Spirit to partner with me in drawing out the hidden wisdom from my spirit, spending time with Him praying in tongues and then asking Him for an interpretation. The interpretation does not always come immediately, but over time it does. The Holy Spirit imparts ideas, thoughts, and images in my soul, enabling me to understand the wisdom of God; this is the same way He will communicate with you.

The Key Is to Persist in Prayer

There must be an interpretation in a church service that accompanies any utterance in tongues. However, when praying in tongues privately, you just need to be open to receiving the interpretation of what you are praying about. The interpretation can come as a word-for-word translation, an impression, a feeling, or a thought. You don't need to worry about how the interpretation will come to you. It may come differently for each person, as we are all uniquely created, and God communicates with us in the way we can best understand.

I used to allocate an hour in my schedule for praying in tongues, but over time, this has changed. I now pray in tongues throughout the day and trust God for the interpretation. The interpretation may come while I am teaching, writing, or spending time with my wife. It could also come as thoughts while at the grocery store or as strong feelings about deciding whether to turn somewhere different while driving. The main point is that your whole life can be constant communication with the Holy Spirit if you make praying in tongues a daily part of your spiritual journey.

There have been times in services when the Holy Spirit told me something about the people present. He even had me call out names of people who had messages from Him, and in each case, the person was there and able to receive the message. All of this happened because of spending time praying in tongues. But remember, these things do not happen overnight. Your flesh and soul may resist dedicating time to praying in the Spirit, and at times, you may question if anything is happening. If you persist and do not give up, the interpretations will start to come. It may take a month, six months, or even a year or more to reach this point.

Accessing the Wisdom of God

The Holy Spirit communicates with people in various ways, as your relationship with Him will be unique to you and may differ from others. While others can mentor and teach you, they cannot dictate the best way for you to develop your relationship with Him. I wish someone had told me this when I began my journey with the Holy Spirit. I didn't have a spiritual mentor and had to learn and grow in my relationship with Him through difficult experiences. This resulted in my early years in ministry basically being spent in the proverbial school of hard knocks.

Your spirit is the part of your being where the mind of Christ resides (1 Corinthians 2:16). Praying in tongues allows you to access Christ, enabling you to pray out the hidden wisdom of God. Every answer to every question you will ever ask is within your spirit, while the Holy Spirit will assist you by providing the words to pray them out. No Christian should ever find themselves in a position where they do not know what to do. Our relationship with the Holy Spirit is the way we reach this place of discernment.

The answers we seek are within our spirits; it is your spirit that prays while praying in tongues (1 Corinthians 14:14). Your spirit prays out the hidden mysteries of God in a way your soul cannot. We spend time in prayer and then ask the Holy Spirit to provide the interpretation (1 Corinthians 14:13). I have found praying in tongues to be the most valuable gift of the Spirit, as it provides a means to access the answer to any question in any situation. I am confident that the Holy Spirit will help you just as He has helped me.

I have grown to the point of praying in tongues continuously throughout the day but did not start that way. It takes time to discipline your flesh and train your soul to sit on the sidelines. The key is consistency; if you can pray consistently for thirty minutes a day, start there. The Spirit will help you, and your time praying will increase over time. Over time, insights will come, and the wisdom of God will begin to flow into your soul.

Every Christian can draw on the wisdom of God. We have the Person who knows everything about every subject living in our spirits. Speaking in tongues is like the bucket you would lower into a well to draw out the water in it. The wisdom is already in your spirit, but you will have to draw it out. This is not something the Holy Spirit will do for you. He will help, encourage, and guide you but will not do the work for you. I have met far too many Christians over the years who were unable to yield to the Spirit in prayer simply because they were waiting for Him to pray through them.

God's Good Gifts

If ye then, being evil, know how to give good gifts unto
your children: how much more shall your heavenly
Father give the Holy Spirit to them that ask him?

LUKE 11:13

The baptism of the Spirit is available to all born-again Christians, not just a select few. Unfortunately, there is a lot of incorrect teaching in the church today that has prevented many people from experiencing all that God has provided for them. According to Luke 11:13, our heavenly Father wants to give the Holy Spirit to all His children, and the only requirement is for us to accept this gift.

God is good, but the church has unfortunately misrepresented Him to the lost and dying. Your heavenly Father desires for you to have the Holy Spirit more than a physical father wants to give good gifts to his children. This is for your own benefit, as God understands that you need help to receive His good gifts, which is why He sent the Holy Spirit. The Holy Spirit entered your spirit the moment you made Jesus the Lord of your life and will be with you through thick and thin.

Ask and the Father Will Give You the Spirit

As you approach the Lord and ask for the baptism of the Holy Spirit, first, you must believe that it is His will for you to have the Holy

Spirit. It is not only His will, but also His desire for you to be baptized with the Holy Spirit. You just need to ask, stand on His promises that the Father will give the Spirit to Him, and then receive.

The challenge people often face in receiving Him is that they are looking for an emotional experience when they receive the baptism of the Holy Spirit. Now, don't misunderstand me. The baptism with the Holy Spirit can be a very emotional experience, but it doesn't have to be. Some people I have prayed for over the years have had the biggest change in their lives without any outward emotional expression. They just reached out and accepted the Spirit by faith. They did not have any form of outward emotional expression beyond opening their mouths and speaking out the language of their spirit as the Spirit gives them utterance.

There was a lady named Marge who was a janitor in a church I once ministered in. I was originally scheduled to speak in one service but ended up spending sixteen weeks ministering for that congregation. Marge would come night after night to the altar for prayer. While other people fell to the floor, ran, or shouted, the janitor, Marge, would just nod, thank us for the prayer, and then return to her seat. The pastor was concerned and set up a prayer group to pray for her and dedicated time to seek God. From all appearances, it seemed as if Marge was resisting the Spirit of God.

Several weeks passed with Marge continuing to come forward each night for prayer. The pastor and I prayed and cried out to God for her to be touched. Intercessors were meeting daily, but still it seemed as if nothing was happening. Our perspective changed one night when Marge asked to give her testimony. She described the work of the Holy Spirit in her heart as peeling away layer after layer of carnal desires. We discovered that night the person who "appeared" to have been receiving the least had undergone the most radical change without any outward demonstration!

You Are Not a Puppet
for God to Control

I want to emphasize that outward demonstrations like running, dancing, or falling to the floor under the influence of the Holy Spirit are not necessary. While these things can happen, they are not essential. Our relationship with the Holy Spirit is a spiritual one. We should seek a deep, meaningful relationship rather than just seeking temporary emotional experiences.

Many people have faced obstacles in their Christian journeys because their focus on physical desires has kept them more connected to the physical world than the spiritual realm. Jesus told His disciples that true worshipers would worship in "spirit and in truth" (John 4:24). This doesn't require us to engage in physical activities like running, laughing, or jumping during service; in fact, I have found that services with fewer physical demonstrations often lead to the highest levels of worship.

Individuals who have experienced significant growth in their relationship with the Holy Spirit are often not visibly demonstrative, not living from one emotional high to another.

Our excessive focus on emotional or physical demonstrations has hindered many in their quests to be baptized with the Spirit. One common misperception I have encountered is the belief that God will take control of their mouths and force them to speak. However, the Holy Spirit longs to partner with us in prayer but will not compel us to speak in tongues. The responsibility to speak is ours alone. The Holy Spirit's role is to provide the utterance, and our part is to speak.

I compare speaking in tongues to ministering under the anointing. The Holy Spirit inspires me when I teach but will not take control and deliver the message. If a minister does not open their mouth, the message will not be delivered. Similarly, if you do not open your mouth to speak, you will be unable to speak in tongues. Let's examine Acts 2:4 for illustration:

> And they were all filled with the Holy Ghost, and began to speak with other tongues, as the Spirit gave them utterance.

In this verse, who spoke? When I ask people this question, most answer and say it was the Spirit who spoke. However, the verse does not explicitly say that the Spirit spoke; it actually says that "they began to speak with other tongues, as the Spirit gave them utterance." Here, "utterance" means the Holy Spirit inspired them to speak; He provides the inspiration, and we speak in tongues.

The Holy Spirit is a gentleman. He will not take control of you, possess you, or force your mouth to move and speak in tongues. There is a ministry gift of tongues that is exercised in a public service, but there is also a private prayer language all believers should be exercising every day. You can speak in tongues at will and do not have to wait for some special anointing any more than you have to wait for an anointing to speak in your native tongue.

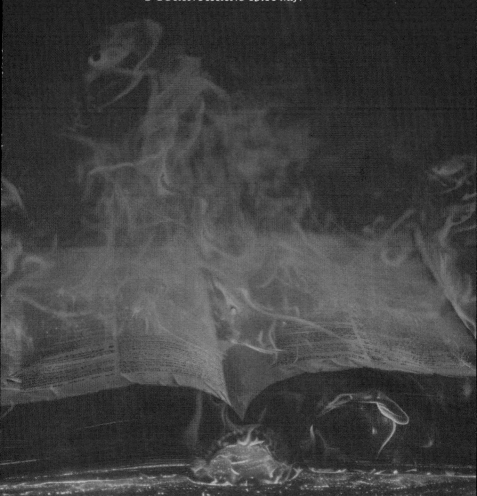

FELLOWSHIPPING WITH THE SPIRIT

The grace of the Lord Jesus Christ,
and the love of God, and the communion
of the Holy Spirit be with you all. Amen.

2 CORINTHIANS 13:14 NKJV

Chapter 29

Are You Listening?

*My sheep hear my voice, and I know them, and they follow
me: and I give unto them eternal life; and they shall never
perish, neither shall any man pluck them out of my hand.*

JOHN 10:27-28

Christians often talk about their struggle with hearing the voice of the Spirit. He is always speaking to us, so that is not the problem, and they are asking the wrong question. The problem is on our side—we have not trained ourselves to identify His voice, which will be the focus of this section. I am going to share what I have learned from the Holy Spirit that has really transformed my relationship with Him.

Every believer in the Lord Jesus Christ should intuitively understand the importance of being able to recognize His voice. There should be no question in any of our minds about this. The Christian who develops a relationship with the Spirit of God will also develop their ability to understand how He communicates with them. This person will also be able to access His wisdom, freeing them from the limitations placed on those limited to their own natural wisdom.

We Need the Spirit to Guide Us

I look back in my life at all the dumb decisions that could have been avoided if I had looked to the Spirit before making choices. You can also probably make a list of decisions that were not the smartest that you made, which probably would not have been made had you looked to the Holy Spirit before. The Bible tells us a child left on their own "will bring shame to his mother" (Proverbs 29:15). In other words, we are not meant to live without the help of the Holy Spirit.

There are many Scriptures we could reference that show the benefit of having the Holy Spirit lead and speak to us. For this to happen, we must train ourselves to recognize His voice. This is what we are going to be discussing in this section of the book. The Spirit desires for you to develop a relationship with Him. As I have previously said, He is only waiting for you to acknowledge Him and ask for His help.

You Can Hear His Voice

Jesus made a statement in John 10:25-30 that is relevant to our study here:

> Jesus answered them, I told you, and ye believed not: the works that I do in my Father's name, they bear witness of me. But ye believe not, because ye are not of my sheep, as I said unto you. My sheep hear my voice, and I know them, and they follow me: and I give unto them eternal life; and they shall never perish, neither shall any man pluck them out of my hand. My Father, which gave them me, is greater than all; and no man is able to pluck them out of my Father's hand. I and my Father are one.

The Lord was referring to His relationship with the body of Christ.

It's evident that He wasn't only talking about the Jews because in John 10:16, He mentions "other sheep," which refers to Gentiles. Jesus was discussing the time after His death, which is the era of the church that you and I are part of. His statement makes it clear that the awareness of His voice is the difference between the saved and the unsaved. As His sheep, we can clearly hear His voice. Jesus also mentioned that we should be so attuned to His voice so that we will not hear the voice of Satan:

> *And when he putteth forth his own sheep, he goeth before them, and the sheep follow him: for they know his voice. And a stranger will they not follow, but will flee from him: for they know not the voice of strangers.*
>
> JOHN 10:4-5

The Holy Spirit is the one who speaks to us. We see this said in John 16:13:

> Howbeit when he, the Spirit of truth, is come, HE WILL GUIDE YOU INTO ALL TRUTH: FOR HE SHALL NOT SPEAK OF HIMSELF; BUT WHATSOEVER HE SHALL HEAR, THAT SHALL HE SPEAK: AND HE WILL SHEW YOU THINGS TO COME.

The Holy Spirit resides within us and constantly communicates with us. Unfortunately, many Christians have tuned their ears more to the voice of the world and its negativity than to the Holy Spirit. The struggle that many face in trying to listen to God's voice should not be the norm. It's abnormal for most Christians to have such difficulty connecting with the Lord and the Holy Spirit. Unfortunately, our spiritual deafness and hardness of hearing are not what God intended.

The Holy Spirit Wants
to Spend Time with You

One of the first things you must embrace to enter fellowship with the Spirit is the fact that you do not have to be a super saint to hear His voice. A relationship with the Spirit is not limited to just those of us who are in ministry. Paul wrote to the entire body of believers in 2 Corinthians 13:14, exhorting them to have fellowship with the Holy Spirit. Every member of the body of Christ can enjoy an intimate experience with the Holy Spirit.

This fellowship is one of the foundational principles of our relationship with the Spirit. Many believers are aware of Him but have a misconstrued idea they are not worthy to fellowship with Him. You need to take this out of the realm of Him limiting His time to only certain people to that of the Spirit desiring to spend time with you. The Holy Spirit wants to speak to you and reveal Jesus to you. He desires to give personal direction in your life, guiding you in each step.

I will come back to this point in another chapter and explain how to hear His voice in more detail. The key point for now is the Spirit is constantly speaking every minute of every day. Every time you come up against any type of a circumstance where a decision must be made and you are wondering what to do, He will always provide the answer. So, the question is not why He is not speaking. Instead, it is why aren't we tuned into Him and listening?

As a result, most are looking for Him in the wrong places and so never enter an intimate relationship that He desires to have with all of us.

The Holy Spirit Will Personally Reveal the Word to You

There are several Scriptures in the Old Testament that prophesy the day we live in as mentioned in the New Testament. They talk about some of the benefits available to us today. The first one is Psalm 32:1-2:

> Blessed is he whose transgression is forgiven, whose sin is covered. Blessed is the man unto whom the LORD imputeth not iniquity, and in whose spirit there is no guile.

In Romans 4:7-8, the apostle Paul quotes verses that discuss a New Testament reality that is accessible to us today. These verses emphasize that our sins have been addressed through the blood of Jesus.

The next verse we'll explore is Psalm 32:8, which pertains to the ministry of the Holy Spirit in the life of a believer today:

> I will instruct thee and teach thee in the way which thou shalt go: I will guide thee with mine eye.

You now have access to the Holy Spirit in a way that was not possible for those living under the Old Covenant. While Abraham, Moses, and David had a relationship with God, they could not experience the same level of intimacy with the Spirit that we can today. Every person who has been born again can develop a relationship with Him and can receive personal teaching from the Holy Spirit. John refers to this in 1 John 2:20-21:

> But ye have an unction from the Holy One, and ye know all things. I have not written unto you because ye know not the truth, but because ye know it, and that no lie is of the truth.

The "unction" mentioned by John refers to the anointing of the Spirit. The Spirit lives in your spirit and is available to teach, guide, and lead you every moment of every day. This can be seen in 1 John 2:27, which tells us that the "anointing we have received abides within us." Every believer has a special anointing from God. When people ask me what that anointing is, they're asking the wrong question because the anointing is a who and not a what.

The Horse and the Mule

I referenced Psalm 32:8, which tells us God promised to instruct us and teach us in the way we should go. He does this through the ministry of the Holy Spirit. Psalms 32 is a prophetical psalm looking forward to the benefits of the New Covenant. David, the author of the psalm, was looking forward to the day we live in and was prophesying about it.

Psalm 32:9 is very important for those desiring to access the Holy Spirit and His ministry in their lives:

> Be ye not as the horse, or as the mule, which have no
> understanding: whose mouth must be held in with bit
> and bridle, lest they come near unto thee.

This passage is a powerful reminder that instead of relying on our circumstances, we should focus on the guidance of the Holy Spirit. Many Christians today prioritize their hardships and problems over the Holy Spirit, much like stubborn horses resisting their riders. The passage uses the analogy of a horse's bit causing discomfort to emphasize that we should not wait for distressing situations to turn to the Holy Spirit for guidance. I have witnessed people suffering due to their choices, which could have been avoided if they had developed a closer relationship with the Spirit and followed His guidance willingly.

At times, I have heard ministers talk about the Holy Spirit using circumstances to lead us. While I agree He will use a circumstance we may have gotten ourselves into as a teaching opportunity, I cannot agree He causes them. You also must understand that even though He can use circumstances to lead us, this is not His preferred way to do so. The number one way we should receive direction from Him is through hearing His voice. Unfortunately, many people do not listen, mostly because they do not know how to. They have not been taught correctly and are often following ministers who themselves have not developed a relationship with the Spirit and do not know how to hear Him.

Chapter 30

Learning to Depend on the Spirit

Be ye not as the horse, or as the mule, which have no
understanding: whose mouth must be held in with
bit and bridle, lest they come near unto thee.

PSALM 32:9

You will not be able to develop a relationship with the Holy Spirit or learn to hear His voice if you can live without Him. That is a straightforward statement that struck home for me the first time I heard it. You are going to have to cultivate a hunger to spend time fellowshipping with the Spirit and hear His voice. This habit is not something that will come naturally, and our flesh and soul do not naturally desire to spend hours with someone they can't see or emotionally connect with.

We saw in the last chapter that we are the Lord's sheep who should be able to know and discern His voice. He was not limiting this to His twelve disciples; every Christian has access to the Holy Spirit and can cultivate a relationship with Him. While it may not necessarily square with your experience, this includes the opportunity of spending time fellowshipping with Him. I have learned He desires to spend time with me more than I do with Him.

The Best Trained Horse

In Psalm 32, David urges us not to act like horses or mules that lack understanding. He explains how well-trained horses respond to their rider's slightest touch without needing a bit or a bridle. Similarly, we can become attuned to the Holy Spirit's guidance through training, even though our flesh and soul may resist.

Psalm 32:9 sheds light on the way many Christians live—pursuing their own desires and only seeking the Spirit's help when faced with challenges. David suggests that we shouldn't live this way; instead, we can cultivate a relationship with the Spirit and cease allowing circumstances to control our lives.

Over the years, I have encountered many people who yearn to discern God's plan but struggle to find it. Instead of nurturing a relationship with the Spirit and heeding His guidance, they frequently switch from one job to another. In most cases, they are unaware that He is with them and desires to guide them in every aspect of life. The idea of developing a relationship with the Spirit is unfamiliar to much of the body of Christ today due to a lack of comprehensive teaching about Him.

A Still Small Voice

Isaiah 30:21 describes the person who hears the Holy Spirit's voice:

> And thine ears shall hear a word behind thee, saying, This
> is the way, walk ye in it, when ye turn to the right hand,
> and when ye turn to the left.

This passage describes the way the Holy Spirit wants to guide us. He wants to communicate with us and share God's wisdom. The Holy Spirit will lead us and help us avoid the snares that Satan sets to make us stumble in life.

We live in a hostile world where Satan is focused on stealing, killing, and bringing destruction into our lives (John 10:10). However, God has not abandoned us. In the midst of chaos, there is a quiet voice. The Holy Spirit is speaking, and He will help you make everything manageable and guide you through each step.

Fellowship Is Not Optional

The Spirit will guide you and help you avoid obstacles. He wants to speak to you and share God's wisdom with you. If you learn to listen to Him, the Holy Spirit will help you overcome any obstacle and get out of the messes you have made in your life. There is no situation that cannot be overcome, for He has the answer to every situation and problem.

All of us must come to a place where hearing the Spirit's voice and following His direction is not optional; this will require dedication and a willingness to discipline ourselves. He will not force Himself into our lives or take control to make us listen to Him. You have to desire these things, commit time to pray, and seek the Holy Spirit. There is no other way to develop our relationship with Him. You must make the choice to set aside time each day to seek Him.

There may be a situation in your life that seems insurmountable. However, it only requires a single word from God to turn any situation around. Receiving that word cannot happen if we do not train ourselves to hear the voice of the Spirit. For this to happen, we must make the choice to spend time listening to give Him the opportunity to reveal Himself.

The Holy Spirit wants to speak to you and wants to impart God's wisdom. The problem is not His willingness to speak to us. Instead, it is our willingness to allow Him time to train us how to hear His voice and follow Him. Are you willing to commit? Many people are not, and you will never become proficient at hearing or following the Holy Spirit if you are unwilling to put effort into it.

The Desire of Our Heart

If you are still having difficulty understanding this insight, you can think of the Spirit's voice in terms of a radio transmission. He is the transmitter, and we are the receivers. Christians often struggle to hear, but the problem is not with the Holy Spirit. He is transmitting. The issue is instead with our receivers. We must fix the receiver on our end before any of us can get to the place of hearing. Fixing your receiver will require you to first get to the place where hearing His voice is not optional. We all want to hear the Holy Spirit clearly, but for most, this is merely a wish they are unwilling to give any serious effort to fulfill.

You have got to get to the point where you desire the things of the Spirit with all your heart. The Holy Spirit will help you cultivate this desire, but He will not do the work for you. Jeremiah 29:11 is a familiar Scripture often quoted by ministers. It is followed by verse 12, and the two verses together provide insight on hearing the Spirit:

> For I know the thoughts that I think toward you, saith the Lord, thoughts of peace, and not of evil, to give you an expected end. Then shall ye call upon me, and ye shall go and pray unto me, and I will hearken unto you.

The verses are about seeking and finding the Lord. They tell us that God can only be found by those who search for Him with all their hearts, requiring a commitment to seek the Holy Spirit for those who want to enter into a relationship with Him. The person who can live without hearing His voice will not.

Seek Him with Your Whole Heart

Many people today express a desire to have a relationship with the Holy Spirit but do not know how to pursue it. The church leaders have not set a good example in this regard. Because of this, it seems like people only call on the Spirit when they are in trouble. We need to change this attitude.

You can develop your hunger for the Spirit of God by seeking Him at all times. Jesus said that those who "hunger and thirst" for the Spirit will be filled (Matthew 5:6). When you truly want to hear the voice of the Spirit, you will. He desires to speak to you more than you desire to hear from Him. The issue is not His willingness to communicate, but rather our desire to listen. In this chapter, I aim to encourage you to cultivate your hunger by taking the time to pursue Him. In the next chapter, we will explore ways to cultivate our hunger and train ourselves to recognize the Spirit.

Chapter 31

Cultivating Our Hunger for Him

Blessed are they which do hunger and thirst after righteousness: for they shall be filled.

MATTHEW 5:6

One of the greatest needs in the church today is a hunger for the Holy Spirit. In most cases, people express a desire to see the Spirit move, but they often lack the hunger required to earnestly seek Him. Many are more focused on the busyness of life rather than spending time with the Word and the Spirit. It's important to note that hunger for the Holy Spirit cannot be developed while sitting in front of the television, at sporting events, or at the movie theater. It can only be cultivated through extended periods of seeking the Spirit, which cannot happen if we are unwilling to shut other things off.

The Desires of the Heart

In Psalm 37:4, it is mentioned that God will fulfill the desires of our hearts. It's important to understand that desires are not restricted to material needs like healing or financial prosperity. They also encompass the longing for a close relationship with the Holy Spirit and to receive divine knowledge from Him. If you long for a deep connection with the Holy Spirit, Psalm 37:4 promises that God will grant that to you.

I once heard a minister say that when it comes to desire, if we do the opposite of what we want to do, we will be following the Holy Spirit; this holds true for a completely worldly Christian. A Christian who does not seek God will almost always think in direct contrast to God's will. Their natural inclinations will consistently oppose what God has provided for them. Let's take the example of giving a tithe and offering to illustrate this point.

Luke 6:38 tells us the way to receive financially is for us to first give an offering. However, this is not the way our natural minds think. The natural mind says if you need more money, then work harder and hoard. You must borrow, scrape, and do what is necessary to get more. Our carnal nature will resist the idea of giving. Thankfully, the biblical path to increase is giving and being a blessing to people; this is exactly opposite of what our natural being will want to do.

The Source of Our Desires

Your desires will change when you begin to seek the Holy Spirit, as He will start to change them as you spend time with Him. It is possible to come to the point of discerning the will of God based on your heart's desires as your relationship with the Holy Spirit grows. This is dependent on us seeking the kingdom of God more than anything else in our lives.

I have never heard the Holy Spirit speak to me in an audible voice. He has guided me at every step as the ministry has grown, but not once has this been done audibly. The primary direction has been through desires in my heart. This is the same way you will receive direction. Your desires will change and grow during times spent seeking God in His Word and fellowshipping with the Spirit.

Someone who is not seeking God and is living in sin will not have desires in line with God's will. They are not submitted to the Spirit because Satan will be the primary influence over the desires of their hearts. Many people begin their Christian journey with desires formed by the world. These will change only in relation to their willingness to commit to spending time meditating on the Word and in prayer.

Remember this: As you grow your relationship with the Holy Spirit, your desires will change. Seeking the Spirit is not about impressing others but about being genuine and true. If you seek the Holy Spirit wholeheartedly, you will find Him waiting to spend time with you. Your desires may initially differ from the Spirit's, but that's okay. They will change as your relationship with Him deepens. Spending time with God's Word and the Spirit will transform your desires. Living a carnal lifestyle, prioritizing worldly activities over spiritual ones, can cloud your desires, so the key difference between spiritual and carnal lives is actually quite simple.

Replacing Your "Want to" with His Desires

The president of my first Bible college started his message on the first day of orientation with a statement that shocked me. He told us that we should allow the people God called us to minister to, to sin as much as they wanted to. The shock in the room after this statement was evident. After a prolonged silence meant to give us time to think, the president went on to say that our job as ministers was to lead people to the Word and the Spirit; it was the Spirit's responsibility to change the "want to." It took time, but I've come to understand the truth in this statement.

I have spent a lot of time seeking the Lord and meditating on Scripture over the years. As I have done this, God has changed my desires. Because of this, I now minister where I want to, write the books I want to, and teach whatever I want to in our weekly program. I do what I want to because my desires have been completely surrendered to the Holy Spirit. He has replaced my selfish "want to" with His desires. The Spirit will help you do exactly what I have done if you are willing to make the commitment I have made to the Word of God and my relationship with Him.

You will find your desires changing in direct proportion to the time spent waiting on the Lord. As I have said many times already, everything comes back to our relationship with Him. Our entire Christian experience reflects the depth of relationship we develop with the Spirit and time spent meditating in the Word of God. If you are unsure about a desire, set aside time to spend with the Holy Spirit to discuss the desire. If the desire grows, you know it came from Him.

You may have habits or even sins in your life that seem unshakeable. I have met people who went to counselors and deliverance ministries who just could not help them find freedom. Every attempt to get free failed until they began to seek the Holy Spirit with all their hearts. Ungodly desires, habits, and sins will fade over time if you commit to spending time each day meditating on the Word and fellowshipping with the Spirit.

Chapter 32

The Presence
and the Plan

For I know the thoughts that I think toward you,
saith the LORD, thoughts of peace, and not
of evil, to give you an expected end.

JEREMIAH 29:11

God has a plan for your life, and it's the Holy Spirit's job to help you discover it. There's nothing in that plan that can hurt you. Pursuing His plan may involve battles, but the victory at the end of each one will make any effort expended to follow the Word and Spirit well worth it. Over the years, I've learned that the key to accomplishing what the Lord has called me to do is simply not to quit. You will have many opportunities to quit, just like I did, but the Holy Spirit will be with you each step of the journey, helping you keep pressing forward.

You don't have to live each day hoping, wishing, and praying that you are doing what God called you to do. It seems like most Christians I have met approach God's plan as if it's a gamble. They don't realize that the Holy Spirit was sent to reveal the plan and guide them step by step. As we have seen, the Holy Spirit is not only with us but also within us.

It is also possible to learn to discern the Spirit's voice and guidance. Jesus told His disciples that we could expect the Holy Spirit to show us things to come (John 16:13), but there's no reason for any of us to be surprised by life's events if we are listening to the Spirit and obeying His directions.

Following the Holy Spirit

You can stand against any opposition with God. There are a lot of comparisons we could make between the children of Israel and Egypt in the context of our relationship with the Holy Spirit. Israel went into the desert when they left Egypt. They came up against the Red Sea, but even that great body of water was not too great of an obstacle for the Holy Spirit to overcome and enable the Israelites to cross through the sea to safety.

Israel faced many difficulties while wandering in the wilderness. Sin caused a whole generation to be blocked from entering the promised land. But God was still faithful and fed them with manna, guiding them by His Spirit through every situation they found themselves in.

Israel had been delivered from slavery in Egypt and led by God into the wilderness. He remained faithful to them even when they turned their backs on Him to pursue their own agendas and sin.

There are a lot of comparisons we could draw from Israel's time in the wilderness. The Holy Spirit was the one who led them out of Egypt, and He leads us out of our spiritual Egypt. The Spirit will faithfully guide us if we keep our spiritual eyes focused on Him, just as He did the Israelites during their journey through the wilderness. I believe if Israel would have just remembered they were following the leadership of the Lord, they would have been able to resist the temptations to disobey God much more effectively.

Delighting Yourself in the Spirit's Presence

The reason why many people struggle in following the Spirit is that they are not sure if they are being led by Him. This assurance can only be found in a relationship with Him, as it requires a commitment to spend time meditating on the Word and fellowshipping with the Spirit. We previously discussed what is said in Psalm 37:4:

> Delight thyself also in the LORD: and he shall give thee the desires of thine heart.

The main message of this verse is that if we sincerely seek the Holy Spirit with all our hearts, He will guide us to the fulfillment of our desires. The key is to focus on developing a strong relationship with Him. If we overlook this detail, then everything else we've discussed so far will be in vain. Putting God first means prioritizing a relationship with Him over the fulfillment of our desires. Unfortunately, many of us have made the mistake of pursuing our desires without acknowledging Him.

In our Christian journey, everything circles back to building a relationship. The Holy Spirit is here to assist us, and many of the challenges we face in receiving from God stem from not recognizing His presence in our daily lives. The more time we devote to being with Him, the more He will place God's desires in our hearts, and we will begin to see them manifest more and more.

Led by Desire

If you seek God with all your heart through His Word and spend time fellowshipping with the Spirit, you will be able to do what you desire. This is because God will influence and change your desires as the Holy Spirit will put His desires in your heart. I can honestly say that I now do what I want to do, but it was not always this way. My desires have been transformed from carnal to spiritual as a result of consistently pursuing fellowship with the Holy Spirit. Your desires will change as well if you pursue Him.

The Holy Spirit will shape your desires as you spend time meditating on Scripture and fellowshipping with Him. He will change your wants and the things you long for. As your relationship with the Spirit deepens, you will be able to trust your desires more and more. Therefore, if you are truly seeking Him and have a desire to do something, go ahead and do it. The devil will not put desires in your heart to serve in church, go to Bible school, or share the Gospel message.

One of the things I did early on in my Christian journey was to do everything that presented itself to me. I volunteered in the church's audio department, children's ministry, and even worked as a church janitor. Step by step, the Holy Spirit led me to these opportunities. He showed me the things I was not called to do and helped me find my calling in each place. My desire to work in audio, with children, and for cleaning the church decreased, but the desire to teach grew significantly in those early years.

The Holy Spirit has molded my desires to fit the plan of God, and He will do the same for you. Everything we do at MB Media Ministries involves seeking God with our whole heart and allowing the Holy Spirit to shape our desires. He gave me the desire to start our weekly television program which airs three days a week, write these books, and travel to teach the Word. I am just acting on those desires, and we are seeing Him open amazing doors as a result.

What Do You Want to Do?

I have encountered many people over the years who have approached me asking for guidance in finding God's will. They are unsure and do not know how to figure out what He wants them to do. When I ask them what they want to do, it usually surprises them the Holy Spirit would guide them through their desires because they are usually expecting something dramatic from Him like hearing an audible voice, seeing a flash of light, or receiving a vision to discover the plan and purpose of their lives. The idea of quietly meditating on Scripture and listening to the Holy Spirit is unfamiliar to them.

There are individuals who have desired to serve in a particular area or pursue other aspirations for years but have never acted on them because they were unsure if God was leading them to do so. Most of them have never been told that the primary way the Holy Spirit guides us is through our desires. These desires can be trusted if you are delighting yourself in the Lord and pursuing His Word. Discovering the will of God always begins with entering the presence of the Spirit and submitting your desires to Him.

Your relationship with the Holy Spirit will be unique to you. Regardless of what it looks like, it will require a commitment of time to spend with Him each day. There will be a cost, but it will be well worth it, begin with being committed to doing whatever it takes to truly enter His presence. If you keep your heart and mind focused on Him, you will find your desires begin to change. They will grow out of your relationship with the Spirit and can be trusted.

So, essentially, the key to following the Spirit is simply keeping your heart and mind focused on God. If you have a desire to do something that seems to grow during your times of fellowship, step out and act on it. Trust the Spirit to show you any course corrections that may need to be made. Isaiah 28:10 tells us that everything in our Christian journey is "precept upon precept, line upon line." Take the first step and trust the Holy Spirit to guide you to the next step through the desires He places in your heart.

Chapter 33

Dividing Between
Our Soul and Spirit

But he that is joined unto the Lord is one spirit.

1 CORINTHIANS 6:17

Have you ever considered what it means to be "one spirit" with the Lord? This was something I had never really thought about until the Holy Spirit drew my attention to 1 Corinthians 6:17 one day. The word translated as "joined" literally means "glued together," something we have discussed earlier in the book. This verse from 1 Corinthians reminds me of 1 John 4:17:

> Herein is our love made perfect, that we may have boldness in the day of judgment: because as he is, so are we in this world.

The phrase "as He is" is translated from *kathos*, which is an adverb that could also be translated as "exactly" in modern language. If you are born again, there is zero difference between your spirit and the Holy Spirit. This is the reason why your natural desires disappear as you spend time with Him and are replaced by His desires. Our natural desires are a function of the soul, as we learn to live from our born-again spirits by spending time meditating on the Word and fellowshipping with the Spirit.

Discerning the Source
of Our Emotions

The Bible is clear about the Holy Spirit having all the attributes of a person. He has emotions, which is evident in the fact that it is possible to grieve Him (Ephesians 4:30). You are one spirit with Him, so, therefore, there should be no difference between your emotions and His. Unfortunately, this is not the case for most Christians, as they live from their souls with little awareness of the spiritual part of their being.

This is something really simple but often misunderstood. I really struggled with the idea of my spirit being joined to the Holy Spirit at first. It seemed like something too good to be true. We talked about how our desires are replaced by His as we seek Him in the last chapter. This occurs as a result of our tuning ourselves to the spiritual realm while meditating on Scripture and fellowshipping with Him. Our spirits are joined to Him, so learning to live from the born-again spirit is the same as learning to live our lives fully dependent on the Holy Spirit.

There is no difference between learning to discern between our spirit and flesh and discerning between God and the devil. God speaks to us through our spirit, while Satan speaks to us through our soul and flesh. He uses things like the lust of the flesh, the lust of the eyes, and the pride of life as his communication tools. The Holy Spirit, on the other hand, uses our born-again spirits as His primary communication tool to speak with us.

Discerning Between
the Soul and Spirit

This may sound complicated, but it really is not. The writer of Hebrews provides us with the answer for this though in Hebrews 4:12:

> For the word of God is quick, and powerful, and sharper than any twoedged sword, piercing even to the dividing asunder of soul and spirit, and of the joints and marrow, and is a discerner of the thoughts and intents of the heart.

This verse teaches us that the Word of God is "living and powerful" and "sharper than any two-edged sword." It can also discern between our soul and spirit, as well as between our thoughts and intents of the heart. This is important because it distinguishes between our soul, which is the mental and emotional part of our being, and our spirit, which is considered the "real us" in the Bible, as mentioned in Romans 8. Our soul is associated with traits like jealousy, bitterness, depression, and discouragement, which are referred to as works of the flesh in Galatians 5:19-21. On the other hand, our spirit is the new creation in us, and it is where the fruit of the Spirit listed in Galatians 5:21-24 reside.

Developing Discernment

Our born-again spirit always produces love, joy, peace, long-suffering, kindness, goodness, faithfulness, gentleness, and self-control, never discouragement. Anytime we feel discouraged, it comes from our souls. Our spirit remains steady, but our souls fluctuate and need constant nourishment from the Word of God to align with our spirits.

In 1 Corinthians 6:17, we learned that our spirits are joined to the Lord and are always in line with God. This is why our spirit always produces what the Bible calls "the fruit of the Spirit," operating in union with the Holy Spirit. By learning to differentiate between the soul and spirit, we can discern the voice of the Holy Spirit, the devil, or our carnal desires.

The Word of God is the tool the Spirit uses to train us in discernment. Our spirits and souls are closely connected, and without a foundation in the Word of God, it's impossible to discern the source of our thoughts and desires. For example, if you have a thought to visit someone, how would you know if it's from your spirit or soul? The ability to discern comes from a relationship with the Holy Spirit and the Word of God. The Word is used to "divide" the intentions between our souls and spirits. Though closely related, we can develop the ability to discern between the two, and the Spirit will help and train us step by step in doing so.

Dividing Between Soul and Spirit

The Word of God is the only thing that can differentiate between the soul and spirit. As previously mentioned, the primary way we receive guidance from the Spirit is through feelings, perceptions, intuitions, thoughts, and desires. It will not be possible to discern if these are coming from the Spirit or your soul if you are not seeking Him with your whole heart. However, if you are seeking God, Psalm 37:4 promises that He will give us the desires of our hearts (as we have learned earlier). So, the first step is to seek the Spirit, but there are also other things we can do along the way.

One way to determine if a desire is from the Holy Spirit or your soul is to examine it with the Word of God. For example, if you have a desire to bless someone financially, there is very little chance that desire comes from the unrenewed part of your soul. Another example would be found in a situation where you get into an argument with a person. Your soul would want to lash out, but in the midst of your negative emotions, suddenly a desire to forgive the other person rises up. That would not be natural and would most likely be a prompting from the Holy Spirit. Verses like Matthew 5:38-40 tell us to turn the other cheek, which validates that the desire to forgive is in line with the Word of God.

The devil will never tell you to do what God's Word tells you to do. He is opposed to God and will often take something that looks like it is from Scripture and lace it with some unbelief to water it down. Satan's goal is to twist and pervert truth in such a way that a Christian will buy into his lies and accept them as truth. If you are grounded in Scripture and have developed your relationship with the Spirit, it will become easy to discern truth from error.

Satan is a liar. If he could speak consistently with the Word of God, then he would not be the father of lies (John 8:44). The Word is truth, and he will always violate it in some way. So, if you want to know if things like thoughts, feelings, premonitions, or intuitions that you have are of God or not, one of the things you need to do is to treat the Word of God like a ruler and put those thoughts up against the Scripture to see if they conform and are consistent with the Word. If they are, then you will know they came from the Holy Spirit, and you can follow them.

Chapter 34

The Holy Spirit and the Word of God

Thy word is a lamp unto my feet, and a light unto my path.

PSALM 119:105

We have covered a lot of material in the previous chapter about discerning the Spirit's guidance. The last point was when you get a feeling, emotion, intuition, or desire for something, and you do not know where it came from, there is a simple way to figure the source out. Simply take the Word of God and use it like a ruler. Put those things up against the Word; if they conform and are in line, they are from the Holy Spirit. He will never lead you in any way that is not consistent with Scripture.

Everything Must Line Up with Scripture

Hebrews 4:12 teaches us that the Word of God divides our spirit and soul. When discerning whether something comes from the Spirit or our soul, we should remember that anything consistent with Scripture is from Him. The Holy Spirit communicates with our spirit in a way that aligns perfectly with the Word of God. Anything that contradicts Scripture is not from the Holy Spirit. It's that simple.

If something goes against God's Word, it's not from the Holy Spirit. Unfortunately, many Christians do not understand this basic truth. For instance, I recently spoke to a lady who argued that the Holy Spirit cannot move without a physical sensation like heat or oil. When I asked her for validation from Scripture, she couldn't provide a single verse and became agitated when I didn't agree with her.

I don't base my beliefs on physical manifestations like heat, gold dust, or oil. Without scriptural support, I cannot accept such experiences. The Word of God is my foundation, and anything that lacks biblical support is not something I can accept. Many people may passionately argue that their experience is from the Holy Spirit, but without Scripture to support it, they are mistaken. Christians often mistake their passionate desires for something generated by the Spirit. While the Spirit may give us desires that ignite passion, being passionate about something does not necessarily mean the Spirit gave us that desire.

Everything Is Built on Relationship

There will be people who read this book who feel so passionately about something that they have allowed their passion to override the Word of God. I have done this in the past, so I know you probably have done it too. The door for things like this to happen opens when we do not give the Word of God and the Spirit their proper place in our lives. As I mentioned in previous chapters, the Holy Spirit is speaking constantly, like the way radio stations broadcast continuously, and just like the station, if we do not recognize the Holy Spirit's voice, we are tuned into the wrong channel.

The acid test for our relationship with the Spirit is seen in the value we give to the Word of God. Those who give it the smallest value are the ones who struggle the most to identify the source of their desires, emotions, and feelings. They cannot tell if these things are from the Holy Spirit or the devil, most often because they have never committed the necessary time to developing their relationship with the Spirit and becoming grounded in the Word of God.

I know there are some who will read these words that will argue it is almost impossible to spend any quality time with the Spirit because they have so many things to deal with in their lives. This is an argument heard far too often in churches. My answer to it is simple: If you are too busy to set aside time to meditate in Scripture and fellowship with the Spirit, you are too busy to enjoy the benefits provided in your salvation through the redemptive work of Christ. It is impossible to break out of the cycle of defeat and destruction without the help of the Holy Spirit.

He Will Lead in Every Situation

The Holy Spirit will lead us through the Word into all that God has provided in Christ's redemptive work. You may ask, what about situations where there is no specific verse to use? For example, the Scripture does not tell us whether we should buy the house on the corner or in the middle of the block. How do we use the Word in a situation like that?

There are many things we can do in situations like this. I may not be able to cover all of them, but I will introduce some options in this chapter. It is vital for us to discuss this because there are many things in our lives that are not explicitly stated in Scripture. As I have already mentioned though, when it is clearly stated in the Word, you should never look beyond that for additional guidance.

The Word of God means exactly what it says. For example, it tells us to honor our mother and father, that our days may be long (Exodus 20:12). We do not need to look beyond this verse; those who do not honor their parents, regardless of the situation, cannot expect to be blessed. This does not mean staying in an abusive household, but even in cases like that, the Holy Spirit will help one find a way to honor them, even if the child had to be removed from a situation for safety. In cases like this, staying and experiencing continued abuse is not honoring your parents.

God's Word Is Our Final Authority

God's Word must be the final, absolute authority in your life, even in situations where it does not specifically address a situation, such as which house to buy. In other words, why should the Holy Spirit lead you through a specific situation not addressed in the Word if you are unwilling to obey the written Word of God? For example, salesmen are often asked to exaggerate the qualities of a product to make a sale. The argument given is that they do not have to outright lie to customers, but instead just add a few details here and there to make their product look better than the competition in the customers' eyes.

In a situation like this, I would point a person to Exodus 20:16, which contains the commandment to "not bear false witness." This would include a lot of business practices commonly found today, including the temptation for a salesman to exaggerate the qualities of their product. No matter how passionate he or she may be about making a sale, it is better to walk away than violate the Word of God. To some, this may seem like a small matter, but it is significant in the eyes of the Spirit and can harden our hearts toward Him, which in turn affects our relationship with Him.

Follow Peace

When it comes to something specific the Bible does not spell out, I always turn to Colossians 3:15:

> And let the peace of God rule in your hearts, to the which also ye are called in one body; and be ye thankful.

Your born-again spirit is constantly producing love, joy, and peace. If you have been distressed, fearful, angry, bitter, or discouraged, it is because you are more tuned to your flesh than your spiritual nature. Paul tells us we are to "let the peace of God rule in our hearts." The word *rule* could also be translated as "umpire." In America, we assign umpires to officiate baseball games, where the umpire's word is considered to be final. When they make a call, the players have to accept it; there will be no opportunity given to argue against any decision made by an umpire.

The umpire often has to make a decision on the spur of the moment. Once they make it, that is final. Colossians 3:15 is telling us that the peace of God is the umpire officiating our lives. Every thought, every desire, every intuition we have needs to be examined in the light of that peace. If we are lacking peace, it is clear the Spirit is not leading us to go in a certain direction or act on a thought. It is better to sit still and miss an opportunity than to act when peace is missing. It may be difficult to discern His peace at first, but if you commit to spending time each day in the Word and fellowshipping with the Spirit, He will help you step by step, the foundation of the Spirit-led life.

Chapter 35

Hearing Him
Consistently Each Day

And I will pray the Father, and he shall give you another Comforter,
that he may abide with you for ever; even the Spirit of truth;
whom the world cannot receive, because it seeth him not, neither
knoweth him: but ye know him; for he dwelleth with you, and
shall be in you. I will not leave you comfortless: I will come to you.

JOHN 14:16-18

Jesus told His disciples that they could "know" the Holy Spirit; this is equally true for all Christians today. The word translated as "know" is *ginosko*, which describes an intimate relationship with another person that grows through personal experience. We can know the Spirit and develop an intimate relationship with Him because He dwells with us and is in us. He is always with us and speaking, but we are not always tuned into Him. I believe it is imperative that every born-again Christian develops an awareness of His presence and gets to the point of being able to hear Him on a consistent daily basis.

Missing the Supernatural in Our Quest for the Spectacular

I recall a time in my life when I would have confidently claimed, "God told me," even though I wasn't entirely certain if He had. However, over the years, as I have dedicated time to meditating on the Word and nurturing my relationship with the Spirit, my ability to hear His voice has significantly improved. The struggles I once faced with discerning His voice are now a distant memory, thanks to the time we have spent together. He is constantly communicating with us, but many of us are more attuned to the ways of the world and consequently struggle to recognize His messages in the world.

I have been emphasizing that there is no issue with the Spirit speaking to us. He is indeed speaking, but our inability to hear Him is due to being tuned into the wrong "station." If you have been fervently praying and seeking the Holy Spirit's guidance but have heard nothing, it's likely because you don't know how to listen, and we have discussed the various listening methods in the preceding chapters.

One factor that often causes us to miss the Spirit's communication is our fixation on the sensational. While it's wonderful to experience the Holy Spirit speaking to us in an audible voice or to feel His presence in a powerful way that leads people to be "slain" in the Spirit and fall to the ground, these occurrences are not the primary ways in which He communicates with us. We all desire to hear from the Holy Spirit through an audible voice, a dream, or a vision, but these are not the most common means of communication from Him.

God's Word Is Our Foundation

The primary way the Holy Spirit communicates with you is through your thoughts and perceptions. He will give you a revelation, and suddenly you will perceive something or have a desire that you didn't have before. As Psalm 37:4 states, if we delight ourselves in God, He will give us the desires of our heart.

The voice of the Spirit is subtle, so it's important to be mindful and not overlook the thoughts or perceptions received from the Holy Spirit. Sometimes you may wonder why you had a specific thought, but it could be the Holy Spirit trying to communicate with you.

There are a couple of qualifications for receiving and discerning the thoughts, perceptions, and desires that are from the Holy Spirit. First, you must be seeking God with all your heart. Additionally, the Word of God must be your standard: any thought, perception, feeling, or desire from the Holy Spirit will align with God's Word. If they don't pass this test, they are either from you or from the devil.

Many Christians struggle to discern the voice of the Spirit because they lack knowledge of God's Word. It's important not to solely rely on pastors or television preachers for spiritual nourishment. While it's beneficial to learn from anointed teachers, it's crucial to spend time daily reading and studying the Scriptures privately. The devil is not impressed with our quoting others, but he will flee from those who speak from a place of revelation.

A More Sure Word

You will never develop an intimate relationship with the Spirit without first becoming deeply rooted in God's Word. It is impossible to follow the Holy Spirit while leaning solely on our own intuition. The written Word is "a more sure word of prophecy" (2 Peter 1:19). Peter wrote this statement to validate the message he had preached as being received directly from the Lord and the Spirit. He ministered from a place of revelation, unlike many ministers in that day, and today, who relied solely on knowledge acquired through self-effort to fill their messages.

Peter also references his experience on the Mount of Transfigura-
tion in 2 Peter 1:17-18. Can you imagine what it would have been like
to be there when the glory descended on Jesus and seeing Moses and
Elijah? That is what happened to Peter. It seems like that would have
been the ultimate experience, but Peter tells us the written Word is
better than a vision, desire, audible voice, or anything else. The Word
is more reliable than any other experience you or I will ever have.

Let God Be True

God forbid: yea, let God be true, but every man a liar;
as it is written, That thou mightest be justified in thy
sayings, and mightest overcome when thou art judged.

ROMANS 3:4

You must come to the point where God's Word is your sole
source of truth. It must dictate, dominate, and control your life if
your goal is to develop a relationship with the Holy Spirit. He will
never trust anyone who has no desire to come to this place. It is
impossible to discern between the Holy Spirit, your flesh, or the
devil without first becoming grounded in God's Word. His Word
is a perfect representation of His nature and character, and He will
never violate it.

Satan is a liar. Jesus even referred to him as the father of lies (John
8:44). He will take a little kernel of truth from God's Word and wrap
it in unbelief and doubt to try and deceive us. The devil even tried
to trick Jesus during the desert temptation by quoting Scripture. If
you are not grounded in the Word of God and have not taken time
to develop your relationship with the Spirit, it will be almost impossible for you not to fall into Satan's trap.

Many people have asked me over the years how to discern whether what we are sensing is from the devil or the Holy Spirit. The simple answer is to develop deep roots in the Word. God sent the Spirit to teach and guide us, so you cannot develop any depth of root in Scripture without His help. Knowledge of the Word gained through self-effort or academic study is not the type of knowledge needed to overcome the enemy's temptations and deceptive strategies. It is only through the Holy Spirit's guidance that we will be able to move beyond head knowledge of the Word into revelation knowledge.

Ignorance of the Word Opens the Door for Deception

As we come to the close of this section on hearing the Spirit's voice, let me encourage you once again to make the Word of God final authority in your life. It is so subjective for us to say, "I feel this is God's leading." How is it possible to trust our feelings, which are sourced in our souls? You must train yourself to measure every feeling, desire, or intuition against the Word of God. We should all keep Paul's warning from Galatians 1:8-9 in mind:

> But though we, or an angel from heaven, preach any other gospel unto you than that which we have preached unto you, let him be accursed. As we said before, so say I now again, if any man preach any other gospel unto you than that ye have received, let him be accursed.

This is a strong statement you should keep in mind. If any thing you believe is a leading from the Holy Spirit does not line up with Scripture, throw it out. This is so simple, and I am amazed it even needs to be said. Unfortunately, a lot of Christians value their church's traditions more than they do the Word. They are good people who love the Lord, but unfortunately they struggle through their Christian journey as the foundation they have built is wrong.

You do not need to take the word of your pastor or any other minister as being final. The Holy Spirit will speak to us through ministers, but we must always take what they say and measure it against the Word of God. We could literally stop the devil in his tracks if every Christian were to adopt the Word as final authority and develop deep roots in it. Satan uses ignorance of God's Word as his number one tool to deceive people.

Jesus told His disciples that knowledge of the truth would set them free (John 8:32). Satan cannot do anything in our lives without first deceiving us; only truth can shield us from deception. The person with deep roots in Scripture who has developed an intimate relationship with the Spirit will be able to resist Satan's efforts to deceive them. My question for you then as we close out this section is: Are you willing to pay whatever price is needed to become deeply rooted in the Word of God and to develop your relationship with the Spirit?

FLOWING IN THE GIFTS OF THE SPIRIT

Now there are diversities of gifts, but the same Spirit. And there are differences of administrations, but the same Lord. And there are diversities of operations, but it is the same God which worketh all in all. But the manifestation of the Spirit is given to every man to profit withal. For to one is given by the Spirit the word of wisdom; to another the word of knowledge by the same Spirit; to another faith by the same Spirit; to another the gifts of healing by the same Spirit; to another the working of miracles; to another prophecy; to another discerning of spirits; to another divers kinds of tongues; to another the interpretation of tongues: but all these worketh that one and the selfsame Spirit, dividing to every man severally as he will.

1 CORINTHIANS 12:4-11

Chapter 36

The Importance of the Gifts

And these signs shall follow them that believe; In my name shall
they cast out devils; they shall speak with new tongues; they shall
take up serpents; and if they drink any deadly thing, it shall not
hurt them; they shall lay hands on the sick, and they shall recover.

MARK 16:17-18

In this final section, we are going to discuss operating in the gifts of the Spirit. I understand that there may be individuals reading this book who question the relevance of the supernatural gifts of the Spirit in today's context. Let me pose a question to you: If Jesus required the gifts of the Holy Spirit and the miraculous power of God to affirm the message He was teaching, why do we believe that we can minister without them today?

The Gospel Message
Is Relevant for Today

There are differing beliefs about the gifts of the Holy Spirit. Some people think that these gifts ceased to exist after the time of the apostles. Others believe that these gifts have been misused, causing many believers to distance themselves from anything supernatural. I want to share some insights that the Holy Spirit has taught me over the years as an introduction to understanding and operating in His gifts.

Many Christians often speak about what God will do for them in the future tense. They do not understand He has already provided everything they will ever need for this life (2 Peter 1:3). This lack of relevance to their daily lives has led many to reject the Gospel message. It seems that there are very few Christians, churches, or ministries today that are demonstrating God's power, and this needs to change. Many of the people the Spirit sends us to minister to are enduring extremely difficult circumstances and are in need of a supernatural intervention. When the church only preaches salvation as a means to have sins forgiven and secure eternity, there will be people who cannot accept the message because they are unable to see beyond their immediate crisis.

In my experience, people do not outright reject the Gospel message; rather, we are not effectively communicating its relevance to their present-day situations. Many people are going through situations that make them feel as if they are living in a "hell on earth." When Christians approach them and offer the assurance of having their sins forgiven and escaping hell when they die, the message is rejected because they cannot see beyond their immediate situation. They are unable to think about eternity and, as a result, regard the Gospel message as pertaining to a future that is impossible for them to consider.

Partnering with the Spirit

The Christian who begins to operate in the gifts of the Holy Spirit will have a message that speaks to the current situations people are facing. In this section, our focus will mainly be on the word of wisdom and the word of knowledge, as these are the gifts I operate in the most. These are the gifts I am most knowledgeable about, but they may not be the ones the Spirit chooses to use in your life. We are all different and will be used in ways that will impact different people. He will use you to reach people I may never be able to.

When you start operating in the gifts of the Spirit, you will begin to see people healed, delivered, and set free in ways that would not be possible in your own strength. However, you can only reach this point by first developing your relationship with the Word of God and the Holy Spirit. The first unbreakable rule of operating in the gifts is that it is impossible to do so in any depth if you have not first developed a relationship with the Spirit. Those who see the greatest levels of power flowing in their lives work in partnership with Him in every aspect of ministry.

For example, when I minister to people under a prophetic anointing, the gift will resonate with them in a way that makes it evident that the minister could not have known the things being shared. All credit will go to God because there is no way the person ministering could know the things being said. The beauty of the Spirit's gifts is that they bring the truths about God from the intangible realm of our future into our present situations.

Flowing from Relationship

I am not trying to minimize the fact that God has made tremendous promises about our eternal reward or that heaven will be amazing. Christ has guaranteed us an amazing eternal future in His redemptive work that was completed when He presented His blood on the heavenly mercy seat. In Christ, we have escaped hell; but even if there were no heaven or hell, I would still serve God. I would still pursue a relationship with Him and expect His gifts to flow out of our relationship. Paul speaks of the fellowship available with the Spirit in 2 Corinthians 13:14:

> The grace of the Lord Jesus Christ, and the love of God, and the communion of the Holy Ghost, be with you all. Amen.

Our relationship with the Holy Spirit brings the power of God into our everyday lives, and I guarantee that it will also make this life infinitely better. It makes life worth living to know He is with us and desires to spend time with us each day. I believe the gifts of the Spirit and all of the supernatural manifestations of God enhance our present-day lives in ways that are impossible to experience without having the Holy Spirit in our lives.

The Full Gospel

If the church were preaching the full Gospel, I really believe we would be attracting many, many more people to the Lord than are being attracted today. In a sense, the message we have been preaching offers nothing more than an escape policy that guarantees when we die, we will not go to hell. While the true Gospel message does give us an escape from hell, it also provides for an abundant life that includes benefits like healing, deliverance, prosperity, and joy.

Our goal in this book is to discover the Holy Spirit. We started with salvation and have built from there a foundation for you to build a relationship with Him that far too few Christians will ever experience. This would not be the case though if we were preaching the full Gospel message and flowing freely in the gifts of the Spirit.

One of Jesus' final commands was to "go into all the world and preach the gospel to every creature" (Mark 16:15, NKJV). He then listed the signs that will flow through the lives of those who believe the message:

And these signs shall follow them that believe; In my name shall
they cast out devils; they shall speak with new tongues; they shall
take up serpents; and if they drink any deadly thing, it shall not
hurt them; they shall lay hands on the sick, and they shall recover.

MARK 16:17-18

This statement is amazing, telling us that every true believer has the right to believe for these signs to flow through their lives and ministries. The question is not whether or not they are for today, but why we are not believing the Gospel message contained in Scripture. This may be a question we would rather not consider, as it places the responsibility on us, but it is one we should all take seriously.

I grew up in a denomination that didn't believe the Holy Spirit was still relevant. They believed He stopped working when the last apostle died. Looking back, I wonder how they dealt with passages like Mark 16:17-18, where Jesus told His disciples that certain signs would follow true believers. These signs are the distinguishing difference between those who believe and those who don't.

Some ministers claim that Mark 16 was not in the early manuscripts of the Bible, suggesting that they don't believe in Scripture. It's as if they are trying to mold Scripture to fit their lack of belief. It may sound harsh, but if you are not operating in the gifts of the Spirit, you have not yet fully embraced belief. I once heard a minister define "belief" as a firm persuasion based on knowledge. The Holy Spirit expanded this definition to include relationship—knowledge gained in relationship.

Once again, it comes back to relationship. Everything in our Christian journey is meant to flow from our relationship with the Holy Spirit. God sent Him to be with us every moment of every day as our guide. His gifts and manifestations are relevant today, but operating in them at the level He desires requires us to first develop a relation-ship with the Spirit and the Word of God.

Chapter 37

Unbelief and the Spirit's Gifts

And these signs shall follow them that believe; In my name shall
they cast out devils; they shall speak with new tongues; They shall
take up serpents; and if they drink any deadly thing, it shall not
hurt them; they shall lay hands on the sick, and they shall recover.

MARK 16:17-18

Jesus promised His disciples that certain "signs" would follow "those who believe." This means that the absence of signs in our services is a result of unbelief; unbelief is a major obstacle to our ability to operate in the supernatural power of the Spirit. Jesus Himself was unable to minister healing beyond what was needed to heal a few minor illnesses in His hometown of Nazareth because of unbelief (Mark 6:1-6). It is convenient in some ways not to believe in the supernatural demonstration of the Spirit's power because not every person will be healed. There are multiple reasons for this, but in every case, the fault will be on our side and not God's. In my experience, unbelief is the main reason why people are unable to receive. They may not be willing to agree with this statement, but it is true, nonetheless.

243

Is It Always God's Will?

I have heard people say that the fact people do not always get healed is proof that it is not always God's will to heal. Let's consider their argument and apply it to salvation. If you have been a Christian for any amount of time, you have met people who have attended church and not received salvation. I have even seen people who were convicted by the Holy Spirit of their sins but still left a service without yielding and receiving salvation. Does this mean it was not God's will for them to be saved?

There are some who say we should not preach healing based on the argument that it is not always God's will for all to be healed, as not everyone receives healing. If we apply their logic to salvation, do you think we should stop preaching salvation? Obviously not. We have all seen people reject salvation, but this does not stop us from preaching the message of the cross and extending invitations for people to be saved. In the same sense, there will always be people who reject the supernatural power of God, but I am not going to stop telling people that the Holy Spirit desires to move in their lives.

There will always be people who harden their hearts toward God; I wish this were not true, but it unfortunately is. This does not mean that we, as believers, will quit telling them about God's love, the cross, and His invitation to salvation. We should never allow people's responses to influence our willingness to continue preaching the truth of God's Word in any area. I believe people do, though, because they are not completely convinced of God's love in their own hearts. The only way to change this is through a daily commitment to meditating on the Word and spending time fellowshipping with the Holy Spirit.

Faith or Foolishness

The discussion about spiritual gifts begins with Mark 16:17-18. Jesus told His disciples that signs would follow those who believe. He didn't specify that this was only for the original twelve disciples or the early church. He simply said that if you believe, you should expect to see devils cast out, to speak with new tongues, and to see the sick healed. There are people who have taken these things to the extreme, causing others to turn away from the Holy Spirit and His gifts. For example, when I was first saved, I read stories about people who handled rattlesnakes to prove Mark 16:17-18. They argued that the snake's poison could not affect a true believer because Jesus said believers could pick up snakes and not be bothered by their bite. This is not what the Lord was talking about, and I personally questioned these people's sanity. Let's take a moment to consider the time when Satan took Jesus up to the pinnacle of the temple during the wilderness temptation:

> *And he brought him to Jerusalem, and set him on a pinnacle of the temple, and said unto him, If thou be the Son of God, cast thyself down from hence: For it is written, He shall give his angels charge over thee, to keep thee: And in their hands they shall bear thee up, lest at any time thou dash thy foot against a stone. And Jesus answering said unto him, It is said, Thou shalt not tempt the Lord thy God.*

LUKE 4:9-12

In an attempt to tempt Jesus, Satan used a quote from the 91st Psalm. While the verses do promise protection, it would have been unwise for Jesus to jump and expect angels to catch Him. This is why He responded, "You shall not tempt the Lord your God." It is reasonable to expect protection in certain situations, such as when Paul was bitten by an asp while putting sticks on a fire:

And the barbarous people shewed us no little kindness: for they kindled a fire, and received us every one, because of the present rain, and because of the cold. And when Paul had gathered a bundle of sticks, and laid them on the fire, there came a viper out of the heat, and fastened on his hand. And when the barbarians saw the venomous beast hang on his hand, they said among themselves, No doubt this man is a murderer, whom, though he hath escaped the sea, yet vengeance suffereth not to live. And he shook off the beast into the fire, and felt no harm. Howbeit they looked when he should have swollen, or fallen down dead suddenly: but after they had looked a great while, and saw no harm come to him, they changed their minds, and said that he was a god.

ACTS 28:2-6

Paul did not purposely pick up the snake. He was adding sticks to a fire when the snake bit him. God protected Paul from what should have been a fatal bite just as He can you and I if something similar happened to us.

The Word Is Our Foundation

There is a fine line between being foolish and acting in faith. The Holy Spirit will help you stay on the right side but cannot do so if you are unwilling to commit time to develop your relationship with Him. People get into trouble because they only give a half-hearted effort to develop their relationship with the Spirit and the Word, turning to Him only when He is needed. You are fighting a full-time devil, and victory requires a willingness to seek God with all your heart.

It is one thing to say you believe God still heals today and totally another to walk out a healing. I have heard of many ministers with powerful healing ministries that could believe for other people's healing but were unable to receive healing for themselves. I have spent a lot of time focusing on time spent in the Word in addition to talking about the Spirit. We cannot just pursue the Spirit because the devil will attack us, and we will be put into positions that require us to demonstrate the power of God.

We see in Mark 16:20 that the Lord worked with the disciples and confirmed the word they preached with miraculous demonstrations. It was through the anointing of the Holy Spirit that the message was confirmed. Once again, the disciples partnered with the Holy Spirit and the Word, resulting in miraculous demonstrations that drew people to Christ. The disciples did not have any advantages over us. We actually should be operating at a much higher level because they did not have the Bible, television, radio, or any other modern means we have.

The Father's Witness

The early disciples didn't have the technological tools we have today, such as radio, television, or the Internet. Despite this, they had a greater impact on the world than the church does today, relying on miracles, signs, and wonders to confirm the preaching of the Gospel message. While we still see miracles in our services, they are more of an exception than the rule, unlike in the early church.

Some ministers argue that we don't need miracles today because society is more sophisticated than it was in the days of Jesus and the apostles. However, this argument seems flawed. Consider Hebrews 2:1-4:

> Therefore we ought to give the more earnest heed to the
> things which we have heard, lest at any time we should let
> them slip. For if the word spoken by angels was stedfast,

and every transgression and disobedience received a just recompence of reward; how shall we escape, if we neglect so great salvation; which at the first began to be spoken by the Lord, and was confirmed unto us by them that heard him; GOD ALSO BEARING THEM WITNESS, BOTH WITH SIGNS AND WONDERS, AND WITH DIVERS MIRACLES, AND GIFTS OF THE HOLY GHOST, according to his own will?

Notice that these verses tell us that God bore witness both with signs and wonders, with various miracles, and gifts of the Holy Spirit. This reminds me of a statement made by Jesus about His ministry, which is found in John 5:31-37:

If I bear witness of myself, my witness is not true. There is another that beareth witness of me; and I know that the witness which he witnesseth of me is true. Ye sent unto John, and he bare witness unto the truth. But I receive not testimony from man: but these things I say, that ye might be saved. He was a burning and a shining light: and ye were willing for a season to rejoice in his light. But I have greater witness than that of John: for the works which the Father hath given me to finish, THE SAME WORKS THAT I DO, BEAR WITNESS OF ME, that the Father hath sent me. And the Father himself, which hath sent me, hath borne witness of me. Ye have neither heard his voice at any time, nor seen his shape.

Jesus Himself said the miraculous demonstrations occurring in His ministry proved He was sent by God and confirmed His message.

Why would we think it should be any different today with the message being preached by the modern church?

The Dinner Bell

If Jesus needed His ministry confirmed, how in the world can we say today that He was lacking or inferior in any way? He was superior to any of us in every way but still needed the miraculous demonstrations to confirm His message. This is the reason I said arguing that these miracles are no longer needed is insane; it is equivalent to saying the church has grown to a level beyond even Jesus.

The Lord used miracles like a bell that just rang and drew people to Him. Yes, the preaching of the Word is more important than the miraculous demonstrations, but this should be confirmed just as it was in Jesus' ministry. Sometimes a person who is suffering with sickness in their body will hear the message. They will struggle to receive, though, if you tell them the Lord can save them but not heal their body. Symptoms may be screaming so loudly they can't hear, except for some form of miraculous relief that God is more than capable of sending, just as He did for so many in Jesus' ministry.

We cannot say we are preaching the Gospel if we are not seeing some form of miraculous demonstrations in our meetings. Unfortunately, the message being preached in far too many churches and ministries today is a watered-down version of the true Gospel. The early church used the gifts of the Spirit to confirm the Word they preached. If they needed their message to be confirmed in this way, why would we think it should be any different for us today?

Chapter 38

Expect Jesus to Confirm His Word

So then after the Lord had spoken unto them, he was received
up into heaven, and sat on the right hand of God. And they
went forth, and preached every where, the Lord working with
them, and confirming the word with signs following. Amen.

MARK 16:19-20

As we mentioned at the start of this section, there are many people today who do not believe in the gifts of the Spirit, with some believing that the need for them passed away with the apostles. I recognize this, so I spent some time in the last chapter making a case for the miraculous being needed in our day. Mark 16:18 tells us that the Lord worked with them and confirmed the Word through the accompanying signs. Jesus confirms the preaching of the true Word of God with the miraculous; this means that the lack of confirming signs is not a sign of our superiority, but instead of our lack in regard to revelation of the true Gospel message.

How the Word Is Confirmed

The confirmation of God's Word doesn't just come in the form of healings and miracles. It can also manifest through other gifts of the

Spirit, such as the word of knowledge or the word of wisdom. Every manifestation of the Holy Spirit listed in 1 Corinthians 12:7-10 is needed today, as they are ways God bears witness to the message being preached. If you don't see any of them manifested, you need to start examining the message being preached.

Anyone can put together a good talk, stand behind a pulpit, and deliver a message. The proof of what they are saying, though, will be in the changes brought to people's lives. These changes can involve the new birth, receiving a personal word from God, or deliverance from a sickness or disease. According to Scripture, the Lord will always confirm His Word with manifestations of the Spirit, such as gifts of healing, working of miracles, and words of wisdom. The confirmation of the message we preach is required to see the permanent change we all should desire in the lives of those God calls us to minister.

One reason the message of the church is not having a greater impact today is that we lack the confirming signs that accompanied the early church's messages. We are not touching people where they live right now. Jesus and the early Christians showed up and healed people's bodies, cast out demons, and introduced people to the power of the Spirit. Today, we show up and preach a message talking about the power of God but do not give the Holy Spirit the opportunity to manifest. We invite people to the altar but give them no proof that God is who He says He is.

A Lifeline Message

We are essentially trying to convince people to commit to a God whom the Bible says they should serve, without giving them a lifeline. Why should they choose to serve Him if He is unwilling to intervene in their situations or touch their lives with His power? This was a question posed to me by the Holy Spirit, and now I am asking it of you.

Jesus provided answers to the blind, sick, deaf, and paralytic: each of them found deliverance from the Satanic oppression that had kept them in captivity. He has given us a message that provides the same answers to the oppressed in our day, but for the most part, we are not preaching it.

I have come to a point in my Christian journey where I question anyone who preaches a message that is not confirmed by manifestations of the Spirit. Anyone can preach a good message, but the proof of what we preach is in the changes it brings to people's lives. One of these changes is the move from spiritual death to life. Salvation can confirm the Gospel, but so can miracles, words of wisdom, words of knowledge, discerning of spirits, and casting out devils.

Many deny the validity of the operations of the Spirit for the days we live in. Some say we have outgrown the need for them, but they are denying a truth of the Word of God. This is one reason why the message of the modern church is not having a greater impact than it could. We are not reaching people where they are because we are preaching from our souls and intellect instead of from revelation knowledge imparted by the Holy Spirit.

A More Excellent Way

Jesus entered a city and healed people's bodies; many chose to follow Him because they were set free. Today, when presenting the Gospel message, we often only offer the opportunity to repeat a prayer of salvation after us during an altar call. There are few reports of people being delivered, set free, and healed in churches today. Our religious traditions have convinced us that these things do not happen, and we tend to label anyone operating in the Spirit's power as an extremist.

We should be preaching the same message that Jesus, Peter, Paul, and the other apostles preached. Before discussing how to flow in the Spirit's gifts, I sense that it would be beneficial to first look at 1 Corinthians 12:27-31, which is often used as an argument against the validity of the miraculous today:

> Now ye are the body of Christ, and members in particular. And God hath set some in the church, first apostles, secondarily prophets, thirdly teachers, after that miracles, then gifts of healings, helps, governments, diversities of tongues. Are all apostles? are all prophets? are all teachers? are all workers of miracles? Have all the gifts of healing? do all speak with tongues? do all interpret? But covet earnestly the best gifts: and yet shew I unto you a more excellent way.

I have often heard these verses used for arguing that the gifts of the Spirit are not valid. They are followed by a discussion on love in 1 Corinthians 13, which is then followed by instructions given by Paul on how to properly work with the Holy Spirit in 1 Corinthians 14.

First Corinthians 13 is commonly called the Love Chapter, sandwiched between two chapters that speak about the gifts of the Holy Spirit. Chapter 12 ends with the statement, "Yet I show you a more excellent way," which is Paul's introduction to his discussion about the love of God. Some people have interpreted this to mean that we do not need the gifts if we have the love of God, but this is an incorrect interpretation of 1 Corinthians 12:31.

Love Is the Foundation

It is possible to operate in the gifts of the Spirit while still living in a worldly or fleshly manner; this statement may come as a surprise. Just because you are using the gifts of the Spirit does not guarantee that everything that manifests is entirely from the Holy Spirit. I will delve into this topic more thoroughly in a later chapter, but it is one of the most common misconceptions. Some people believe that anyone operating in the gifts of the Spirit is completely surrendered to Him. However, we all have fleshly desires, and Satan will attempt to interfere in order to corrupt the flow of the Spirit. Therefore, every word, action, and thought must be evaluated in accordance with the Word of God.

Let's consider the example of preaching or teaching. The minister may be anointed, and most of what they say may be inspired by the Spirit. However, they are speaking through their own personality, with their own mistakes and failures, all of which influence the revelation being shared. The same applies to the gifts of the Spirit. They flow from our renewed spirits but then need to pass through our souls and unredeemed flesh. Our humanity is not set aside when we yield to the Spirit in prayer or ministry. The Holy Spirit must work through it, so elements of our personality will always influence how we operate in His gifts.

Chapter 39

Do We Still Need the Gifts?

Charity never faileth: but whether there be prophecies,
they shall fail; whether there be tongues, they shall cease;
whether there be knowledge, it shall vanish away.

1 CORINTHIANS 13:8

I have heard many ministers over the years argue that these verses above prove the gifts of the Spirit have been done away with. Their argument is based on the fact that Paul said prophecies and tongues will "vanish away." The verse also states that knowledge will also "vanish away," and those who adhere to this argument never seem to address the fact that knowledge obviously has not "vanished" today. Daniel even prophesied that "knowledge shall be increased" in the "time of the end" (Daniel 12:4), which is the day we live in.

That Which Is Perfect

Those who use 1 Corinthians 13:10 to argue that spiritual gifts are no longer needed tend to focus on the statement, "When that which is perfect has come, then that which is in part will be done away." They argue "that which is perfect" refers to the written Word, which we have, and the early church did not. I agree the Bible is perfect, but it is not the perfect thing Paul was talking about. You can prove that from the verses that follow:

> *When I was a child, I spake as a child, I understood as a child, I thought as a child: but when I became a man, I put away childish things. For now we see through a glass, darkly; but then face to face: now I know in part; but then shall I know even as also I am known. And now abideth faith, hope, charity, these three; but the greatest of these is charity.*
>
> 1 CORINTHIANS 13:11-13

These verses are not a metaphor or an allegory. Paul was referring to the time when the Lord returns, and we receive our glorified bodies in his reference to "that which is perfect." At that time, there will no longer be a need for speaking in tongues or prophesying. Until then, we need the gifts of the Spirit to fulfill the plan and purpose of God for our lives. We still need prophecies and speaking in tongues for the day you and I live in.

The Gifts Are Needed Today

It is certain that we do not know everything. In 1 Corinthians 13:12, it is mentioned that we will "know just as we are known" when we see the Lord "face to face." Instead of proving that the gifts of the Spirit are no longer needed, the verses in 1 Corinthians 12 and 13 actually do the opposite. They prove our need for the miraculous today, just as much as Jesus and the early Christians needed miracles to validate the Gospel message.

Paul encouraged the Corinthian believers to "desire earnestly to prophesy, and do not forbid to speak with tongues" (1 Corinthians 14:39, NKJV). It's hard to argue that spiritual gifts such as prophecies and speaking in tongues are not valid for us today when the Corinthians were told not to forbid anyone to speak in tongues.

In context, Paul is talking about all nine of the manifestations of the Spirit listed in 1 Corinthians 12. These manifestations are for us today, and we will not reach the place of effectual ministry God has ordained for each one of us to walk in without them. We need the gifts of the Holy Spirit to manifest today, to confirm the Word of God, and to draw people to the message that Jesus loves them. This is a powerful truth that far too many Christians have missed, and the Holy Spirit wants us to rediscover it.

Relationship Is Our Foundation

In the previous chapters, we established a foundation for our discussion on the gifts of the Spirit. Our first encounter with the Spirit is at the new birth, and then we deepen our relationship when we are baptized with the Holy Spirit and speak in tongues. This experience opens the door to intimacy with Him, and it is out of that intimate relationship that we flow in the gifts. Everything in our spiritual walk grows out of our fellowship with the Holy Spirit.

The Holy Spirit and His gifts mean much more to me than just doctrine. I have spent countless hours alone with Him over the years and have developed a close relationship with Him. Some people have tried to argue with me based on their doctrinal beliefs, but they have always failed. Relationship will always be more important than doctrine and theology. Doctrine is impersonal and based on knowledge gained through self-effort. Relationship, on the other hand, is personal and built only through time spent with the Spirit of God. You will struggle with the supernatural as long as your understanding of spiritual things is built solely on doctrine.

My personal testimony is the result of the time I have spent meditating on Scripture and communing with the Holy Spirit. There is no difference between me and you; the Holy Spirit desires to spend time with you just as He has with me. Our world needs the supernatural power of God. You can activate the gifts of the Spirit by simply making a commitment to spend time alone with Him every day in your life and ministry. He is waiting for you and is ready to teach you and guide you into everything God has planned for your life. The question is not His willingness, but instead it is yours to commit time to spend with Him each day.

We Need the Power

Our society today is in need of the supernatural power of God, as the church has become too focused on intellectualism and strange practices. There are entire denominations that are calling evil good and good evil. We require the gifts of the Spirit, but we also need to relearn the deeper aspects of the Spirit. Much of what we consider revival today can be likened to a shallow pool with children playing in it. It's time for us to stop playing and move into the deeper waters of the Spirit. The Spirit is waiting and will guide us every step of the way.

I have witnessed the power of God raise people out of wheelchairs, give sight to the blind, and restore hearing to the deaf. These were not miracles that could have happened based on my own ability to deliver a sermon. They required me to be completely reliant on the Spirit, which in turn required me to spend time with Him. Once again, everything we do in life and ministry should stem from our relationship with the Holy Spirit. Pursuing the things of God without acknowledging and pursuing a relationship with the Spirit leads us into intellectualism and strange practices.

How Does He Operate?

The first step to understanding the operation of the Holy Spirit is to comprehend what we commonly refer to as His gifts. Paul provides us with a list of these in 1 Corinthians 12:7-11:

> But the manifestation of the Spirit is given to every man to profit withal. For to one is given by the Spirit the word of wisdom; to another the word of knowledge by the same Spirit; to another faith by the same Spirit; to another the gifts of healing by the same Spirit; to another the working of miracles; to another prophecy; to another discerning of spirits; to another divers kinds of tongues; to another the interpretation of tongues: but all these worketh that one and the selfsame Spirit, dividing to every man severally as he will.

Please take note that Paul refers to these as "manifestations of the Spirit"; they are the things the Holy Spirit does and not necessarily gifts that He gives us. I won't argue about this, but it's something you should consider. The Spirit will manifest differently through me than through you. I often see the word of knowledge, word of wisdom, and prophecy manifest through my teaching, while you may see gifts of healing and the working of miracles operating in your life. There may be people who operate in a similar flow to me but have a different perspective. This doesn't mean I'm right and they're wrong. Everything needs to be judged by Scripture. Many people have gotten into trouble because they don't understand this basic truth. We are far too quick to dismiss people who don't seem to agree with our favorite preacher.

The Holy Spirit speaks through people and flows through them according to their personalities. I am pretty laid back in my teaching, while other ministers love to scream and shout. We are different. God created us this way because there are people who will receive from me who would never receive from a person who screams and shouts. There are also people who would think I am boring and would prefer the screamer. Once again, we are all unique and created in such a way to reach certain people.

There are different gifts and different manifestations: all come from the Holy Spirit. He will show you your place, but first you will have to commit time to spend time meditating in the Word and fellowshipping with Him. We will balance each other out if we will all start by developing our individual relationship with the Word and the Spirit. The Lord is returning soon, and it will take all of us working together to gather in the final harvest of souls.

Chapter 40

Diversities of Gifts

Now there are diversities of gifts, but the same Spirit. And there are differences of administrations, but the same Lord. And there are diversities of operations, but it is the same God which worketh all in all. But the manifestation of the Spirit is given to every man to profit withal.

1 CORINTHIANS 12:4-7

I have emphasized in the first few chapters of this section that the gifts of the Spirit are not optional; they are necessary. Our impact on the world today has been limited because we have separated the Gospel message from its power. Paul addressed this to his critics in 1 Corinthians 2:3-4 when he said, "I was with you in weakness, in fear, and in much trembling. And my speech and my preaching were not with persuasive words of human wisdom, but in demonstration of the Spirit and of power" (NKJV). He used the gifts of the Holy Spirit to confirm the truth of what he was preaching.

The Kingdom Expressed in Word and in Power

Paul was highly educated and could have easily crafted sermons to impress people. In 1 Corinthians 4:18-21, we see his commitment to minister in power compared to many who had become lifted up in pride:

> Now some are puffed up, as though I would not come to you. But I will come to you shortly, if the Lord will, and will know, not the speech of them which are puffed up, but the power. For the kingdom of God is not in word, but in power. What will ye? shall I come unto you with a rod, or in love, and in the spirit of meekness?

Paul had already argued with the Corinthians and tried to reason with them, but with no results. In these verses, Paul is basically telling them that anyone who has not seen the demonstration of power following their ministry as he had should stop talking. Today, we might say he told them to "Put up or shut up!" I think that is a very valid way to deal with things, don't you?

One of the problems we have when it comes to gifts of the Spirit is we have different styles and religious traditions. Some people are extroverts while others are quiet and calm. As mentioned in the previous chapter, the Holy Spirit may inspire two different manifestations of the same gift based on the vessel through which He is flowing. As Paul tells us in 1 Corinthians 12:7, "The manifestation of the Spirit is given to each one for the profit of all" (NKJV). In the end, every gift of the Spirit is given to us for the "profit of all" we minister.

God Has Given Gifts to All Men

God gives gifts to every man but not every person discovers the gifts He has given to them. This is an important point: You do not have to beg, plead, or wait on God to give you any gifts. This is a mindset which seems to have permeated the church, and it is wrong. There are gifts and anointings in all our spirits that need to be discovered. God is waiting for us to discover and activate His gifts while we plead and cry out for Him to give them to us.

The list of gifts given in 1 Corinthians 12:7-10 is not exhaustive:

> But the manifestation of the Spirit is given to every man to profit withal. For to one is given by the Spirit the word of wisdom; to another the word of knowledge by the same Spirit; to another faith by the same Spirit; to another the gifts of healing by the same Spirit; to another the working of miracles; to another prophecy; to another discerning of spirits; to another divers kinds of tongues; to another the interpretation of tongues:

Additional gifts are listed in Romans 12:6-8:

> Having then gifts differing according to the grace that is given to us, whether prophecy, let us prophesy according to the proportion of faith; or ministry, let us wait on our ministering: or he that teacheth, on teaching; or he that exhorteth, on exhortation: he that giveth, let him do it with simplicity; he that ruleth, with diligence; he that sheweth mercy, with cheerfulness.

The Holy Spirit can manifest in various ways today. In 1 Corinthians 12, we see operations such as gifts of healing, working of miracles, and faith. Romans 12 adds additional gifts to this list, such as ministry, teaching, and exhortation. The Spirit's gifts have been distributed throughout the body, and now He is waiting for us to cooperate with Him in their operation.

Don't Put the Spirit in a Box

We each have a place and opportunity to partner with Him. He will manifest through you differently than through me. We have all been created uniquely by the Father, and the Holy Spirit will use our differences to enable us to reach the world. This will enable you to reach different groups of people than I will be able to. In this section, we are going to focus primarily on the word of wisdom, word of knowledge, and prophecy because those are the gifts manifesting in this ministry.

You will have specific ways the Spirit manifests through you, but this does not mean He will not use you in any other area. I have been in services where there were people present who needed a miracle more than a word, and so the Holy Spirit used me to deliver it. I have seen the blind receive sight, deaf ears open, and people come out of wheelchairs. It is awesome when these things happen, but in my ministry, they have only occurred in a small number of instances compared to the gifts I normally flow in.

He Is Always Ready to Manifest

One common misconception about the gifts of the Spirit is that they only operate as He wills. Many Christians "wait" for Him to move, but the Holy Spirit is always available and eager to minister to people. He is simply waiting for us to position ourselves to work with Him; this requires us to shut things off and set aside time to spend with Him. If you do this and tune yourself to His frequency, His gifts will begin to flow.

God always has more revelation, encouragement, and greater depths of His love for us to explore. The Holy Spirit was sent to lead us into the depths of spiritual truth but is often hindered from doing so because of our carnality. He will not force us to develop tender hearts toward Him; it is always our choice to pursue His presence or not. I do not believe any serious Christian will ever purposely choose not to pursue God, but many unknowingly do so through daily decisions.

You will be unable to consistently flow with the Holy Spirit if you think His gifts come and go as He pleases. This is a common teaching today, but once again, He is always available and willing to manifest through us. We are the sole reason there are not more manifestations of His gifts in our lives and ministries. With this truth, I believe you are starting to understand this and are ready to make a commitment to pursue a relationship with Him that will form the foundation for His gifts to begin manifesting fully in your life.

Chapter 41

The Best Gifts

Now you are the body of Christ, and members individually. And
God has appointed these in the church: first apostles, second
prophets, third teachers, after that miracles, then gifts of healings,
helps, administrations, varieties of tongues. Are all apostles? Are all
prophets? Are all teachers? Are all workers of miracles? Do all have
gifts of healings? Do all speak with tongues? Do all interpret? But
earnestly desire the best gifts. And yet I show you a more excellent way.

1 CORINTHIANS 12:27-31 NKJV

In the previous chapter, we discussed how the Holy Spirit works through our individual personalities. The way He uses me to deliver a word of knowledge or wisdom may not be the way He uses you. There is room for differences in the body of Christ. I have observed that people struggle in learning to flow with the Spirit because they try to copy others without realizing that there are no formulas for us to follow. Those who flow the most in His gifts are the ones who have paid the highest price to develop an intimate relationship with the Holy Spirit.

The Holy Spirit does not follow a cookie-cutter model when He forms us. The manifestation of His presence is available to all who have

been baptized with Him, but not all are accessing what has already
been provided to them. The gifts of the Spirit do not just come and
go. When the Holy Spirit deposits a gift in your spirit, it is resident
on the inside of you, and you will be able to function in it at any
time. We do not need to wait on the Holy Spirit, but instead should
be pursuing knowledge of what He has already placed within us.

The Holy Spirit Is Always On

I once knew a man who operated in the gifts of healing. He saw
many people healed but then had an instance in his church where
a little boy died. The pastor told me that he waited on the Spirit to
direct him, but he never received anything, so he did not pray for
the child. That is not the way the gifts operate. You do not have to
be moved supernaturally to go pray for somebody. If you have a gift,
you can use it at any time a need is present. The boy died because
his pastor was too timid to step out and operate in the gift given to
him by the Spirit.

You do not have to wait for the Holy Spirit to activate any gift.
He is always available and waiting for us to become tuned to Him.
Once again, this goes back to the concept we have talked about so
much in this book—relationship. If you set aside time each day to
spend with Him, you will move into a position of receptiveness. This
is the point where you will be able to use the gifts He has given you.

Discovering the gifts that have been placed in your spirit requires
the help of the Holy Spirit. He will reveal them to you, but doing so
requires a willingness to spend time with Him. You have to desire
to discover them, to get to know Him, and to have the Spirit reveal
them to you. This is the beginning of walking in the miraculous. He
will reveal them to you, and then you will have to step out and allow
Him to teach you how to operate in the anointing on your life.

Partnering with the Spirit

Remember, the operation of the gifts of the Spirit is dependent on trust. I have mentioned before that everything stems from our relationship with the Holy Spirit. Just as in the natural realm, it is impossible to fully trust someone you don't know well or only have a casual relationship with. Utilizing His gifts, anointing, and power requires us to initially learn to rely on Him, which, in turn, necessitates us to nurture our relationship. This, in turn, requires a commitment to set aside time each day to spend with Him and to meditate on the Word of God.

Let me use my teaching gift as an example. The Holy Spirit does not take control of me when I sit down to record a program or stand behind a pulpit. He doesn't seize control and compel words out of my mouth. This is not how any of His gifts work. Some people mistakenly believe that the Spirit takes control and that every word, syllable, and action is purely from the Holy Spirit. Some even believe we must reach a point of zero carnality, zero flesh, and zero self to be used by Him.

That is not how the gifts of the Spirit function. The Holy Spirit does not literally control you and make you do something. Instead, He inspires you. He gives you discernment, a feeling, or an intuition. There are various ways to describe them. You take what the Spirit gives you and express it through your own personality. For example, when I teach, I don't sit and wait for Him to take over. I don't pray for a special anointing. Instead, I will sit in front of the camera or stand behind a pulpit and speak.

God has given me a gift, but I have to spend time seeking the Lord in His Word and communing with the Spirit to develop in it. I teach according to the wisdom imparted during my time with the Spirit, but that wisdom flows through my personality. The Holy Spirit has given me a message, but it is delivered through my personality, my knowledge, and my understanding. This is a very important truth that is often overlooked in the church today.

Discerning the Heart

Recognizing that the Spirit uses our personality has really helped me not only in my ministry but also in how I approach other ministers' messages. The Holy Spirit has taught me to look beyond just the words being spoken when listening to messages. I try to listen for the heart of what they are saying and not just every individual word or the religious style used.

I have heard people criticize ministers for being technically incorrect in one or two points. In most cases, they were right. The minister made a mistake and said one or two things that were incorrect. He or she may not have said it correctly, but their heart was right. You must never forget that the Holy Spirit does not give us a word-for-word transcription of what to say while teaching or preaching.

The Holy Spirit provides the message and the discernment to receive it. For example, when I pray for someone, the Spirit does not give me, word for word, things to say. I might discern they are discouraged and pray for them to be encouraged. The Holy Spirit might give me insight into their need for a revelation of God's love. He provides the framework, but then I have to draw on the wisdom received during my times of meditation in the Word or fellowship with Him to fill it in.

We are human beings, and our souls must be renewed with the Word of God. If the heart of what is being said is right, we must look beyond the words being spoken. In the process of delivery, I might say something that is actually wrong. We are all growing, and you will make a lot more mistakes at first, but this should not stop you from stepping out. The Holy Spirit is patient, and He will help you develop in His gifts. You will never get there though waiting for everything to be just so before being willing to step out and allow Him to use you.

Made in the USA
Columbia, SC
09 January 2025

49904635R00164